D1243947

READING, HOW TO

Books by Herbert Kohl

Reading, How To
Age of Complexity
Language and Education of the Deaf
Teaching the Unteachable
36 Children
The Open Classroom
Anthony Cool as Golden Boy

READING, HOW TO

HERBERT KOHL

E. P. DUTTON & CO., INC. | NEW YORK | 1973

Published simultaneously in Canada
by Clarke, Irwin & Company Limited, Toronto and Vancouver

SBN: 0-525-18895-9

Library of Congress Catalog Card Number: 78-158608

For Antonia, Erica, Joshua, and their friends

ACKNOWLEDGMENTS

I want to thank the following people who contributed to the making of this book:

David and Delores Spencer; Lisa and Orlando Ortiz; Cynthia and Jim Brown; John Holt; John Fitzgibbon; Arnold and Susan Perkins; Lawrence and Marcie McGaugh; Thalia Kitrilakis; Kathy Sloane; Jean Jessner and the people at the New Schools Network; Horace Upshaw, Bill Collins, and the late Buddy Jackson of Black House; Liz Avakian and Susan Bement of Berkeley Community High School; Hank Heifitz, Billy Hunter, Jane Hewitt, and a few years ago, Ana Luks, all of Odyssey; Welvyn Stroud; Allan Kaprow, John Harwayne, Betsy Barker, David Conley, and Daryle Totty of Other Ways; the staff and parents at Kilimanjaro House; and the other teachers in public and free schools in the Bay Area who have worked with me over the last five years.
Special thanks are due to Carmen Alegria, Victor

x   READING, HOW TO

Acosta, Isabel Alegria, Maria Rosa Grunewald, and those
other members of the staff of La Casa de la Raza in Berkeley who tried some of the ideas in this book.

H.K.

PREFACE

There is no reading problem. There are problem teachers and problem schools. Most people who fail to learn how to read in our society are victims of a fiercely competitive system of training that requires failure. If talking and walking were taught in most schools we might end up with as many mutes and cripples as we now have non-readers. However, learning to read is no more difficult than learning to walk or talk. The skill can be acquired in a natural and informal manner and in a variety of settings ranging from school to home to the streets. The conditions for natural learning are minimal and certainly not mystical or technically complex. Reduced to basics the following are sufficient to enable people to acquire the skill of reading as well as develop the ability to perfect that skill:

1. a person who knows how to read and is interested in sharing that skill, and who has

2. a nonelitist, noncompetitive attitude toward sharing knowledge and information as well as

3. some understanding of the process of learning to read and

4. a belief that reading is an important human activity that the young should master;

5. pencils or pens, writing surfaces and printed material if possible;

6. a context for learning in which learners feel secure enough to make mistakes and ask questions;

7. respect for the culture and mind of the learner and therefore an ability to understand and use what the student brings to the situation; and finally

8. patience, a sense that there is time to learn.

There are two more conditions that apply specifically to the learner who should have

9. the ability to use some language as well as reasonably intact senses and

10. a desire to read or at least curiosity about reading.

These conditions need elaboration and in paraphrased form provide the structure for this book.

CONTENTS

READING, HOW TO

CONDITION 1:
WHO IS QUALIFIED TO TEACH?

Anyone who reads with a certain degree of competency can help others who read less well. This is the case regardless of age or previous educational training. However most people in this culture are not accustomed to thinking of themselves as teachers. This is especially true of students in school who undervalue each other's capacity to share knowledge and skills and look to the adult teacher as the source of all learning.

Teaching is supposed to be a professional activity requiring long and complicated training as well as official certification. The act of teaching is looked upon as a flow of knowledge from a higher source to an empty vessel. The student's role is one of receiving information; the teacher's role is one of sending it. There is a clear distinction assumed between one who is supposed to know (and therefore not capable of being wrong) and another usually younger person who is supposed not to know.

It is possible however to think of teaching in another way, as more akin to guiding and assisting another person than to pouring knowledge into him or her. When a baby is learning how to talk, he or she is surrounded by innumerable guides who have mastered the skill to a greater degree than the baby, but none of whom know all there is to know about talking.

There are four people in our family in addition to me: my wife Judy, my daughters Antonia who is five and Erica who is three-and-a-half, and my son Joshua who is a year and a half. Josh is learning how to talk and he has four teachers on different levels of competency with the language themselves. Because Judy and I have a greater mastery of spoken English than Erica or Antonia does not mean however that we are more effective teachers of Josh. The girls spend a lot more time playing with Josh than we do and he follows them around and talks to them all the time. They sometimes seem to understand him a lot better than we do.

I notice they correct him every once in a while or name objects for him and ask him to repeat the words. It is a game for the most part but they want to communicate with him and he wants to communicate with them so there is a natural reason for them to guide and assist him with language, and for him to accept their help.

The girls are also learning how to read in a natural manner. There are a lot of books around our house and the kids see the adults reading and want to do it too. Josh picks up a book and pretends to read. So do Antonia and Erica, only in different ways. Tonia knows which side is up or down, how the pages turn, and how the writing moves across the page. She's heard us read some books so often

that she feels she can read them herself and does in a way
—moving her finger across the page and reciting the story
she knows by heart.

She also knows the alphabet and some words.

Erica knows which side of the book is supposed to be
held up, but forgets which way the pages turn and the
writing goes. Tonia helps her and sometimes reads the
stories she has memorized to Erica who follows avidly.

Erica on the other hand helps Josh turn the book right
side up, talks to him about pictures, imitates Judy or me
reading a story.

Whenever there is a question about a picture or a word
the kids bring the books to one of us and we tell them.

Judy and I in turn are still learning how to read—she has
begun to read texts in ethology and has a new technical
language to figure out. I am trying to make my way through
Paolo Freire's *Pedagogy of the Oppressed* and have to learn
his special use of some words as well as the meanings of
some of his statements in the original Portuguese, a language I do not know. I have to deal with a translation and
learn whether the translation distorts Freire's thoughts.

With the exception of Josh, we are all teaching and
learning reading at different moments in our lives. There
is no one of us who is always a teacher or always a learner.
In fact the children often teach us to look at something differently—a story or picture, which they see more clearly
than we do.

The other day I came upon Tonia and a six-year-old
friend sitting in her bedroom reading a simple comic book.
He was teaching her what he learned in school—pointing
out words, reading sentences, explaining the story. He remembered what he picked up in school and being just a

first-grader saw nothing wrong with sharing that knowledge.

Many of us underrate what we know or forget how we learned ourselves and therefore do not believe in our capacity to teach. We are trained to believe that professionals are the only ones who can teach, and that teaching requires a school. We are afraid to teach our children to read, or to teach other people's children to read because we might mess up the work of professionals. We deny that professionals fail even when we see it happen and allow ourselves to believe that, rather than the professional being wrong or incompetent, our children are failures.

Of course professionals, in order to maintain their special claim to teaching or law or medicine, encourage our feelings of inadequacy and incompetence. They even develop ingenious ways of covering up their own mistakes as well as the hollowness of many of their claims to expertise. For example, there is a new category of diseases that doctors have chosen to call "iatrogenic diseases." Translated into simple language "iatrogenic" means doctor-caused. The iatrogenic diseases consist of health problems people develop because of doctors' mistakes and include ailments ensuing from side effects of drugs or aftereffects of surgery or mistakes in diagnosis. To call those ailments "doctor-caused" is to place responsibility where it belongs—that is, with the doctor. To call them "iatrogenic" legitimizes the doctor's errors and assimilates them to other disease categories such as cardiovascular diseases. Instead of a doctor's admitting that he made a mistake or didn't have adequate knowledge, he can tell his patient, "I'm afraid you have an iatrogenic disease," thereby locating the problem with the patient and creating the impression that he has a professional understanding of what is wrong.

I am surprised that educational professionals haven't followed their medical cousins and avoided dealing with problems they create for children by creating a new category that would appear to explain away teacher-caused learning problems. It would be easy! The Greek for teacher is *didaskalos*. "Genic" is the suffix used to express the idea of "being caused by" or "giving use to." Put them together and neaten it up a bit and we have "didagenic learning problems." Imagine parents being told when their child is failing to learn how to read, "I'm sorry but your child has a didagenic learning problem" and then being assured that the same professional who caused the problem can cure it.

The process of "professionalizing" ignorance is very common in our culture, which is obsessed with credentials and the power they can provide. Teaching need not be the province of a special group of people nor need it be looked upon as a technical skill. Teaching can be more akin to guiding and assisting than to forcing information into a supposedly empty head. If you have a certain skill you should be able to share it with someone. You do not have to get certified to convey what you know to someone else or to help them in their attempt to teach themselves. All of us, from the very youngest children to the oldest members of our cultures should come to realize our own potential as teachers. We can share what we know, however little it might be, with someone who has need of that knowledge or skill.

If you are in a position to help someone, it frequently helps to remember how you learned something yourself. This doesn't mean imitating your teachers so much as looking at the process of learning you went through, often despite your teachers. It also helps to listen to the learner's questions carefully, to discover the kind of help someone wants from you. For example, people may want you to tell them how to read a particular word because they want to learn how to sound out complicated words in general, or they may want to know it because the meaning of a story they are reading hinges on the sense of that word. In one case they are asking for a lesson, in the other for a quick answer.

It is important for the person who teaches to learn how to respond appropriately.

Occasionally you should take inventory, think about what you know how to do, and about ways of sharing those skills. People complain of isolation and powerlessness in our society. Teaching is a form of connection for the teacher as well as a gift to the learner. One doesn't have to become a "teacher" in order to go about teaching. Look around and devise ways to share what you know.

I remember a fantasy I had on the subway in New York when I was in the fifth grade. I was reading some complicated book that had some words I couldn't pronounce or understand. There were many people in the car reading the *Daily News* and *The New York Times*, and I wanted to ask someone to help me with the words but was scared. My fantasy was of being punched, stomped, laughed at, ignored, and ridiculed for daring to ask a stranger for such help. I don't think I'm alone. We are accustomed to asking strangers for directions if we're lost, but to ask for help with reading or the mastery of some skill is often looked upon as an invasion of privacy and a threat or challenge.

Somehow we must all open up to the possibility of being teachers, of assisting each other and not holding on selfishly to the little we know or undervaluing that knowledge.

Students in schools can teach as well as learn—we all can and without elaborate or expensive training. Reading can be taught by anyone who has learned up to the level of their competency.

This is not to deny, of course, that some people will be more obsessed with reading or the teaching of reading than others, nor to deny that there are different levels of competency. However one need not be an extraordinarily gifted reader to bring others to the point of being able to teach themselves on as complex a level as they want.

CONDITION 2:
KNOWLEDGE AS AN
EXPENSIVE COMMODITY

Learning to read is often just an incidental by-product of what traditional schools attempt to teach. A main goal of schooling in our society is to get the young to the point of conforming to a competitive mode of functioning in which being first is identified with being best and in which the failure of some is considered a natural event in human history. Consequently, students have to learn not to share what they know because that might lose them a competitive edge over other students. They also have to learn to compete for the teacher's attention and affection and turn the acquisition of skill and knowledge into an elaborate game in which there are winners and losers.

The traditional American classroom is governed by the teacher with the aid of an elaborate series of controlled so-called learning devices that enable the teacher to know at every moment what every student is supposed to be doing.

It is up to each child to learn for him or herself. No student is responsible for the learning of any other person and students are encouraged to look down upon the slowest or least compliant learners. The teacher's methods, which usually come from a prepackaged developmental or basal reading program,* are assumed to be effective for the "serious" student. If a youngster fails to acquire the skill or comply with the rules for learning, he or she is considered retarded or criminal, that is, in more polite school language, a learning or behavior problem.

Failing to keep up with the pace prescribed by the program and set by the teacher is an indication of inferiority. Because the teacher has a rigid notion of rate of progress, it is natural to form reading groups with moral biases built in—a "slow" group, a "normal" group, and a "fast" group. The notion that different individuals learn *normally* in different ways and at different paces is difficult to fit with the notion that there is a right way of learning.

There are other moral biases built into the traditional, teacher-centered classroom. Not only is the good student one who performs well for the teacher, but also the child learns to read in order to show he or she is a good student (and by association a good person). The central motivation for learning is not the acquisition of the skill and the self-fulfillment reading and writing can bring. Rather it is the approval of the teacher and of one's parents. Good readers are often good citizens, though of course in many

* The same critique applies to completely individualized structured reading programs as to group programs. They all predetermine what a student must do and attempt to manipulate the student into following directions and trying to move faster and faster along a prescribed path. Their goal is generally to produce students who make good scores on standardized reading tests rather than develop sensitive, socially and politically aware readers.

traditional classrooms there is the bizarre phenomenon of some students reading too well—that is of moving faster than the teacher wants and asking too many penetrating questions. A teacher-centered classroom turns issues of learning and the development of skills into questions of approval and rejection. It is no wonder then that many students who conform and learn as they are told end up resenting the price they have had to pay and avoid using the skills they acquired in schools. This is especially true for white middle-class kids who acquiesce to the demands of their teachers and parents and believe in the rules:

> I am a good student
> Therefore I am loved (good).
> I am loved (good) because
> I am a good student.
> I will be a good student
>   so I can be loved (good).

and fear the consequences of nonconformity:

> I am a bad student
> Therefore I am not loved (bad).
> I am unloved (bad) because
> I am a bad student.
> I will be a bad student
>   so I can prove that I am unloved (bad).*

When love, approval, moral status, competitive ability, and the acquisition of a skill are so compounded in the classroom, it is no wonder people come away from the experience of schooling resenting what they learned.

Since most of our schools are middle class in culture and

---

* With apologies to R. D. Laing and his *Knots*.

dominated by white middle-class values and people, it is no wonder that many poor white and nonwhite people fail to learn the basic skills of reading. If a student is not ready to play the love/hate game with the teacher, if the teacher does not identify with the student and therefore doesn't care if he is good (that is, doesn't care to love him or her), if in addition the whole system of learning is based on a series of rewards and punishments that denigrate the values and lives of the students' parents, then it is no wonder that many of these students reject the whole business of confusing acceptance, rejection, competition, loving, and learning.

Some students (predominantly from the middle class) do learn to read within the traditional classroom and others learn despite it.* For the former, the pace the teacher sets is natural and the love offered for conformity to the teacher and competition with one's peers rewarding. The substance of the reading program probably doesn't matter much for them—any one that keeps them working regularly and rewarded periodically will do. The problem is what happens when the teacher disappears—will there be any other reason for them to read, or will they feel, as many American adults feel, that reading is a chore rather than a source of pleasure and a vehicle for learning all one's life?

The question of how reading is to be taught is a moral one, and not just a matter of finding the proper technology. This can be seen even more clearly by looking at the remedial reading clinic, which is a good illustration of what

* Many people who learn despite school are quickly engaged in reading outside of school once they master some minimal skills in school. Comic books and romances specifically written for the young become their texts and reading becomes an activity that they engage in for themselves and not for the sake of the teacher or the grade.

the traditional school system does with students who are considered failures.

The remedial reading clinic fits within the moral world of the traditional classroom. A remedy according to the *Oxford English Dictionary* is "a cure for a disease or other disorder of the body or mind" or a "means of counteracting or removing an outward evil of any kind." In many of our schools students who have not learned to read by traditional methods are considered to have a learning disease or be vested with some form of evil that must be removed or remediated. These students are removed from their classrooms for a few hours a week and sent to a special room designated as a reading clinic and staffed by someone who is supposed to be a specialist in reading—the educational equivalent of an internal medicine man or orthopedic surgeon or psychiatrist. The clinic is set up differently than a classroom. In many remedial reading situations there are a few chairs or desks placed around a teacher's desk. A well-stocked clinic will have many books, programed reading material, workbooks, material designed to develop perceptual skills such as hand-eye coordination and left-to-right orientation. There will be a wide variety of resources available so that the specialist will be able to develop an individual or small-group program that will make the sick student well by getting him or her to read on grade level and therefore be able to return to the classroom and fit into the regular reading program. The prime goal of remedial reading is to prepare the student to fit back, not to enable him or her to read well. Therefore the "good" remedial reading teacher must believe in the culture of the school. If not, he or she will be considered a disruptive maverick whose attempt to help the kids read well will be taken as an attempt to disrupt the culture of the school.

Students are "referred" to remedial reading as patients are "referred" to mental hospitals. They do not go by choice and are not released until they are deemed well. In the public elementary schools at which I have taught the kids going to remedial reading felt they were dumb, or at least they felt that other people thought they were dumb. Some welcomed the opportunity to get better and return to compete with the rest of the class. Others gave up on themselves altogether and looked at remedial reading as an hour's release from the constant humiliation they experienced in the classroom. None of them thought very much about reading as a skill to acquire for their own strength and purposes—they were that much caught up in being the victims of the social and moral system we build around the acquisition of the simple skill of reading.

Many remedial reading teachers use an elaborate diagnostic procedure to analyze everything from the student's reading ability to his or her dietary habits to the state of the soul. The only thing left out is an analysis of what the student's teacher had been doing to induce failure. For example, the Gates reading diagnostic form includes the following information:

Age, grade, intelligence
   Chronological age
   Grade status
   Binet IQ
Silent reading tests
Oral reading
Vocabulary
Reversal test

Phrase perception

Visual perception techniques

Auditory techniques

Tests of vision

Tests of hearing

Observations or tests of speech

Eye movements; use of finger; lip movements; head movements, etc., in silent reading

Evidence of emotional tension, fear, irritation, lack of confidence, etc.

Evidence concerning special interests and distastes

Influence of home, parents, and other out-of-school factors

School history

Some useful information can be acquired by using this elaborate procedure, but the medical setting—the implication that the student is sick—tends to create nervousness and encourage some of the psychological problems it is meant to cure.

The assumption that a student needs remedial help if he or she has not learned to read needs to be examined. First of all, if someone has not acquired a skill there is nothing to remediate. To need remediation, strictly speaking, the skill must be either acquired in a confused manner or acquired then lost. If a person who has not learned how to read is simply considered as someone to be taught or helped for the first time, the whole problem of guilt or failure disappears and with it the need for a special place to deal with failures. There are some cases where there is a genuine need for remediation, such as cases where people lose previously acquired ability to read through head injuries.

Even these cases can be confounded by overreligious adherence to a medical model and to the school's notion of success and failure.

Several years ago I worked with a sixth-grade girl who had a severe reading problem. She was referred to me by a doctor after many reading specialists had given up on her. The girl had read perfectly well during her first four years of school, but when she was ten she was involved in a serious car accident. Her head was thrown against the dashboard and she had suffered severe headaches ever since. Also, she seemed to have forgotten how to read, though her verbal and mathematical abilities were completely intact. This seemed a clear case of someone who needed remedial help.

When I first saw Lillian she was thoroughly demoralized. She had recently scored 2.7 on a reading test and had to score at least 5.0 to be promoted to the seventh grade, and thus go on to junior high school with her friends. She was sure she would be left behind in the elementary school and put in a "dumb" class to boot. That was what her guidance counselor had told her.

I asked Lillian to read Maurice Sendak's *Where the Wild Things Are* (Harper), one of my favorite diagnostic tools. The language is simple; the story is sophisticated; the pictures are interesting and a bit scary. In the middle of the book there are six pages that contain only illustrations, no words. This gives me an opportunity to ask questions about the story and the pictures, which can lead to an interesting talk about wildness and the symbols Sendak uses to embody it. After a little talk I can get a sense of how much interpretation and elaboration the reader is used to.

Lillian read the first few pages with no trouble (there are only a few lines per page). On about the fifth page she made a simple mistake, read "mild" for "wild," a word she previously had no trouble with. Immediately after making the mistake she panicked and read every other word on the page incorrectly. I noticed she looked away from the page, wrinkled her brow, and began to make sound associations that had nothing to do with the story. For example, she read "more" as "four" and then said "door," "boor," "coor" and finally trailed off into some inaudible sounds.

I asked her to stop for a while and rest. She began again and was fine until she made another mistake. Then the same flight from the written page occurred.

Lillian didn't have any problem with phonics. She knew how to read in a technical sense. Only she could not sustain herself for more than a few sentences. She had no stamina and didn't know how to help herself when she made a mistake.

I spoke to her about my observations, and she was surprised. She was used to going to remedial reading clinics, getting a "work-up," and then being given a reading treatment. No one had ever spoken to her about the process of reading, or about what they felt were her problems. She had been treated as a sick child, incapable of understanding her own problems, and was usually told to do exercises that made no sense to her.

I worked with Lillian for two hours a week over a period of three months. She wanted to learn to read again, and I saw no reason she couldn't learn. For the first few weeks we talked about her problems. Every time she made a mistake we stopped and talked about how she could check herself. After a while she could stop when she made a mistake and start again. She found that slowly counting to five helped calm her down after a flight of sound associations. There was nothing mystical about her problem or "professional" about its resolution.

It turned out that Lillian had a problem focusing her eyes on the written word. I didn't need a test of perceptual skills to see that, it was only necessary to look at her. I suggested she follow along the page with her finger, and it seemed to work during the lessons at home. It created serious problems at school, however. Her teacher refused to let her use her finger while she read. Somewhere he had picked up the notion that it was a bad thing to do. The remedial reading specialist agreed. I spoke to the teacher about it. He could not give me any reason why reading with one's finger on the page was wrong or harmful, so he referred me to his supervisor, who took the same position in the same irrational way. Finally, I had to get a doctor's note and threaten a lawsuit to enable Lillian to read in school in a way that was obviously helping her.

Lillian and I did a lot of stamina training. I explained to her almost everything I knew about reading, and together we planned out a reading program she could follow by herself. She learned to control her nervous habits and her tendency to panic disappeared. She used her finger and sometimes a piece of paper to help her focus. Together, we practiced taking reading tests. By the end of a few months she could read again and could also understand what reading problems were all about. She could, and did, help other students with reading problems.

In June she was given a reading test again and scored on a sixth-grade level. The teacher and the reading specialist refused to accept the results. They said that progress could not be made that quickly and therefore Lillian and I must have cheated.

They retested her, and she scored the same. They refused to accept the second test results either. They gave her a third test, and she scored on the fifth-grade level. Some of her nervous habits had begun to return. The school was beginning to create a new reading problem for Lillian. Again, with the help of a doctor and the threat of a lawsuit, we got the school to accept the results of a fourth testing on which Lillian managed to score on the fifth-grade level. She was promoted to junior high.

Lillian's story illustrates how school can actually inhibit young people's learning how to learn. The example, though dramatic, is not such an exception as it might seem. Lillian was nervous because of her accident. But she was even more nervous over the prospect of not being promoted. She was separated from her friends and put into a class for "special" students because she couldn't read. She took tests, and nobody believed her results, thereby undermining her confidence and making reading more of a problem. And there was no way for her to escape the situation because the law says that she has to go to school, and her mother cannot afford a private school or a special tutor.

In this case the remedial reading clinic was no more successful than the regular classroom. That's not surprising since their goals are the same—fit the child to the system of learning without bothering to find out how the child learns best.

I have thought a lot about my experience with Lillian and about what specifically helped. Nothing was done to her in a medical sense. No technical knowledge was employed though I had some experience watching young people read and helping them develop programs based upon what I could perceive about their approach to written material. There was no way Lillian could fail so far as I was concerned. As long as she wanted to learn how to read we would keep on exploring strategies together. Eventually, we were bound to hit on something that worked. If not, I would ask a friend to help. Lillian was not a failure, she was just seeking a way to learn how to read again.

The attitude of the person who assists another is crucial in the teaching/learning situation. Teaching a skill such as reading is not a phenomenon that can be abstracted from the values of the teacher or the institution the teacher works for. If you believe that learning is a competitive phenomenon that is bound to produce failure, some people must be put in the position of being designated failures in order to justify your beliefs. If, on the other hand, your concern is to help people acquire the power necessary to control their lives, failure is your failure as a teacher and not the pupils'. In our culture there is a competitive elite. That is, a group of people who succeed in beating others at academic or financial games. The victorious have no responsibility to share their knowledge or wealth with the defeated. In fact, they need the presence of the defeated to justify and verify their victories.

If one cares to help people read, to share one's own skills, then the phenomenon of failure on the part of students is out of order. You can help some people; others you may not be able to assist but some other person might. To separate reading from competitive gaming implies a generosity toward others, an offering of one's own skills and wealth to people who do not have them. It implies that the other has a right to refuse the gift without being considered inferior or a failure; it also means that the person who learns is not expected to be in the obligation of the teacher or the institution that employs the teacher. If a person learns to read the only responsibility one can hope of them, and the greatest at the same time, is that they will assume the obligation of teaching someone else to master what they have achieved.

CONDITION 3:
UNDERSTANDING SOMETHING ABOUT
READING (AND A DESCRIPTION
OF AN ALTERNATIVE TO
STANDARDIZED TESTING)

People who want to teach reading must understand something of the process of reading though there is that rare person who is able to help others learn without thinking much about it. I have looked through the literature on reading for a direct, nonjargonized description of what little is known about the process of learning to read and haven't found anything. Most writing about reading is bound to the assumptions that (1) the skill will be acquired in a traditional graded classroom, (2) there is an appropriate amount of material to be learned each month of the school year by the normal child,* (3) there is *a* develop-

* Hence the notion that there are measurable grade levels in reading and that the statement that someone reads on a 6.7 level in seventh month of the sixth grade has specific meaning in terms of reading skills and understanding.

mental sequence or order in which the skills of reading must be acquired, and (4) teaching reading should be the province of trained and credentialed professionals. However there is no reason to assume that reading must be learned in a traditional classroom, or that learning moves along a smooth path with measurable amounts of knowledge absorbed over specific time periods, or that there is one way of learning or even a best way. There is even less reason to believe that teaching should be anyone's special province.

It is important to have a sense of the different ways in which people learn to read and also to acquire ways of finding out how well someone actually reads. In order to help people do these things I have organized what I know about reading into a schema that can be used to analyze how well people read as well as develop learning programs for them based upon the analysis. Before describing the schema I must give several warnings:

1. I am not presenting *THE* way one must look at the process of reading. It is my way based on my experience at present.

2. There is no claim that the schema is complete. Hopefully others will add to it and modify it on the basis of their own experience.

3. The schema does not imply any particular way of teaching or any context in which learning must take place. It is an attempt to set down the various skills that go into the process of reading as well as some of the psychological and social dimensions that contribute to learning to read. It also does not imply that all the reading skills must be

learned in the order they are presented. This is not a developmental reading program.

4. Finally, the schema is not designed for credentialed teachers or reading professionals. It can be easily understood and used by anyone who can read this chapter, and can also be explained to students who are trying to learn to read. I believe it is crucial that learners have a clear sense of what they are supposed to be learning and of how learning can take place so that they can teach themselves to the greatest degree possible.

A way of looking at reading

Levels
Beginning
Not Bad
With Ease
Complex

I have broken down the skill of reading into four different levels of competency. It is possible to define three levels or five or seven or any number instead of four. However in my experience these levels describe differences I have perceived in people's ability to handle different types of written material. They do not pretend to be the only way to look at reading competency. The levels have been labeled: (1) beginning, (2) not bad, (3) with ease, and (4) complex.

LEVEL 1: BEGINNING READING

Everyone in our culture is constantly exposed to written material through billboards, television, packages, product labels, street signs, graffiti. Many words are learned informally and in specific contexts such as on a cigarette pack or beer can or on the body of a car. People who want to learn how to read, and this includes young children as well as adults, bring a whole range of experience with the printed word to the learning situation. Some know the whole alphabet but only a few of the sounds the letters represent; some know sounds very well but may confuse certain letters such as p and q or b and d. Others may have a familiarity with picture books or comic books or photo magazines and others might have no experience with books. Some may be able to write or at least recognize their own names and the names of many friends as well as a few charged words like "kill" and "live"; "pussy" and "dick." Generally in school all of this informally acquired knowledge is considered of no value, and the beginning reader is thought of as having no knowledge whatever of the written word. This immediately removes learning from previous experience and knowledge, and does not build on the learner but rather processes the learner through a predetermined and often alienating course of study.

From the perspective presented here a beginning reader is someone who has had no formal instruction in reading (or as in the case of too many students, has had bad school experiences and turned away from formal school-based instruction) but whose experience with the written or printed word might be considerable.

The beginning level of reading *incorporates* what the learner has picked up informally and adds to that certain skills and an articulated sense of what the processes of reading and writing are. When a reader is ready to move beyond the level of beginning reading he or she should be able to: (1) know about the way printed material is oriented on the page, (2) have a command of a basic vocabulary of words acquired on the streets or related to the social, political, and personal realities of one's life, (3) have a memorized vocabulary consisting of words that appear frequently in writing and bind thoughts and sentences together, (4) know the alphabet, (5) have a pretty good grasp of most of what is called phonics as well as an awareness of how sounds blend with each other to form words, and (6) have the ability to read simple sentences, newspaper headlines, street signs, and uncomplicated directions.

Let me consider these skills a bit more:

Levels	Skills
Beginning	1. Knowing print 2. Known words 3. Words that connect and words that place 4. Alphabet 5. Sounds and conbinations of sounds 6. Simple sentences
Not Bad	
With Ease	
Complex	

1. Knowing Print

In order to read books or other printed material as they are produced in our culture it is necessary to be familiar with a few things. First of all it is important to know what is right side up. Then it is important to know that pages turn from right to left and that the text reads from left to right and top to bottom. It is finally necessary to know that words are the units of meaning and that there are greater spaces between words than between letters in the same word. These simple facts are the goals of reading readiness programs. In many schools a year is spent on trying to teach the concepts of up and down and left and right and forward and backward to children, even if they already know the concepts, in order to transfer that knowledge to the experience of reading. In my experience all of this knowledge, which has a lot to do with the familiarity young and older people have with books, can be directly explained rather than taught indirectly.

My three-and-one-half- and five-year-old daughters want to know how books should be read; they ask me to tell them the right way to do it and I do it. Imagine the confusion that could be created if in response to asking how to turn pages I insisted they first *tell me* the difference between left and right and up and down. A lot of energy can be saved by answering questions directly and on the level they are asked, rather than trying to reduce them to a series of structured lessons that avoid the immediate question because you might not think the reader is prepared to understand your answer. It is better to assume the learner is intelligent and find out the opposite than vice versa.

A simple way to help learners get familiar with the orientation of print in our system of writing is to code a few books with arrows, eyes, and hands so that, for example, the front page looks like this:

The eyes indicate the direction of print on a page, the hand how to turn the pages. A few books coded this way will give the student a way to teach him or herself how it is done. Similarly, a copy of the alphabet indicating what is considered right side up through arrows can be of use to some students and a sentence with words underlined

↑ A B C D E F - - - - - - - X Y Z ↑

can help to illustrate the units in the sentence. However, often these crutches are not necessary and it is best to use as few as possible.

An important question arises for the teacher in the case of all the skills to be described in the program. How do you find out what the student knows? The easiest way of course is to ask. However, sometimes that route is not possible. There are other more indirect ways: observe how students approach written material, how they leaf through books, or how their eyes pass over the page. Ask them to pick a story for you to read to them and watch how they hand you the book. Do they know where to begin?

The person who teaches must become a highly skilled, not too obtrusive observer. Paper and pencil tests or formalized questioning are not necessary in diagnosing how well someone reads. Most people will answer you directly if you ask in a concerned, unthreatening way. What people cannot or will not tell you about their ability to read, you can find out by observing how they deal with printed material.

Diagnosis can be turned into a threatening situation if you play teacher or doctor, asking people what they know, recording that information, and then passing on to the next question. Diagnosis and teaching should be fused as much as possible. For example, if someone tells you they don't know which way pages are supposed to turn and therefore that they can't tell the front from the back of a book, don't just record that information and return to it at a later date—ask the student if he or she wants to know and tell them or give them a way of finding out. Take every opportunity you can to give your students knowledge, hints, and techniques that they can use to teach themselves. Make learning as simple as possible.

2. Known Words

Words Brought by the Student

People in our culture recognize a number of words just by being exposed to them constantly. EXIT, STOP, OPEN, CLOSED, BLACK POWER are some examples, though there are people who can recognize "stop" in this context and

not in this one: STOP

It is important to discover how many words a person knows before any instruction begins. There are several ways to do this. Walk around the student's neighborhood or trace the route the student follows from home to school or work each day. Copy down all the words you encounter including graffiti, street signs, billboards, names of stores or schools. Then add to that list the student's name as well as the names of as many relatives and friends you can discover. Write up the list in two forms, one that indicates the context and the other with the words only:

| 106 Street | 106 Street |

| FOR RENT | FOR RENT |

Add to this a series of products that the student uses and utilize the packages (including cigarette packs, beer cartons, phonograph record jackets) in a similar way:

the package   in print only

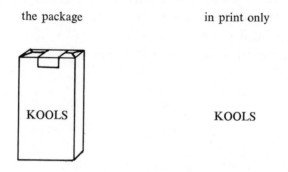

KOOLS   KOOLS

Find out how many of these words are known by the student by asking him or her to read the package and context words at one time and the list at another. People's names of course will just be listed. It is also possible to get this information informally by making up the lists with the learner.

For younger people it is sometimes fun to turn the whole business of diagnosing and discovering the informal vocabulary into a series of games. First there can be *guessing games*: look at the word, guess the meaning. *Matching games*: match the word with the package it belongs on. *Sorting games*: for example, pick out all the cigarette brand names in the list, or all the girls' names, or all the car names.

While playing these games, the students will not only be revealing what they know to you, but also will be learning new words and providing you with an opportunity to observe how they learn.

This knowledge of how people learn can be used in designing programs for them. For example, if you observe that some students are sounding out words while others are guessing wildly or stammering nervously, you know something about these students' strengths on the one hand and needs on the other.

Here is a sample of informal words the staff of the primary school of La Casa de la Raza in Berkeley, California, used to discover what words their students knew outside of school, as well as samples of the context cards they made:

Gloria	Coke
Monica	Private
Keep out	Albert
Closed	Larry
David	Rogelio
Michael	Francyn
Jorge	Gracie
Hector	Gus
Oscar	Yvonne
Juan, Jr.	Maria Theresa
Store	Walk
Push	No
Cafe	On
One way	Off
Ladies	Enter
In	Exit
Sixth	Tenth
Kool	Bus
Salem	San Pablo
Don't walk	Pull

Stop	Out
Ford	Cold
Nardo	Hot
Chevrolet	For sale
Danger	Open
No parking	For rent
Men	

It is not enough, however, to know what printed words students bring to the learning situation. It is important to use these words as a beginning place for teaching and self-teaching. Many things can be done. For example:

1. Have the students enlarge their list, wander the neighborhood and learn to read their streets more consciously.

2. Teach sound combinations (or what is usually called phonics) using as beginning words the informal word list. Students can learn to play with and vary product names and at that same time learn how words are put together. For example:

KOOLS can be varied to

FOOLS since cigarettes kill, to

TOOLS since they are used as tools to control nervousness, to

TOOLESS since they disarm you, and so forth.

More abstract games can be played, too, varying parts of words or substituting letters:

STREET	to
MEET	to
MEAT	to
SEAT	to
TREAT	back to
STREET	

It is possible for learners to use the knowledge they bring with them to the learning situation as a tool to help them to understand some of the ways in which the printed code works and to practice reading.

3. Develop writing exercises using the informal words in various combinations, so that out of names, signs, graffiti, slogans, etc., poems can be created. A few years ago, Victor Hernandez Cruz and I experimented with the possibilities of developing language games that involve what we call *minimal poetry* and utilize the knowledge of words students bring with them to the learning situation.

These games were inspired by several developments in contemporary poetry. Recently, many poets have been experimenting with *concrete poetry* and *found* or *pop poetry*. Concrete poems use the physical shapes of letters as well as the meaning and sound of words, and usually build a physical picture as well as a verbal one. A concrete poem can consist of the word "apple" repeated over and over again in the shape of an apple. Or it can consist of a transposition of a single word into several other words that resemble it. An example of the latter is the following poem by Bob Cobbing, which appeared in Emmett Williams' *Anthology of Concrete Poetry* (Something Else Press, New York)*:

* Reprinted with the permission of Something Else Press, copyright © 1967.

grin
grin
grin
grin
grim
gay green
grey green
gangrene
ganglia
grin
grin
grin

A concrete poem may also play with dividing familiar
words in unexpected ways. I wrote a series of concrete
poems entitled:

myco
ncre
tefa
mily

One of the poems was "Mother":

other
o the mother
her

One of the basic characteristics of concrete poetry is
that it evolves from simple elements that can be repeated,
changed and used in other complex ways. (*Once Again,*
edited by Jean-François Bory, New Directions, is worth
looking at, as well as Emmett Williams' anthology.)

Found poetry (and one of its variants, pop poetry) dif-
fers from concrete poetry in that it uses verbal elements
found in everyday life and recombines or rescans them in

such a way as to develop new perceptions of old and familiar verbal experiences. For example, found poetry can utilize street signs, snatches of conversations, the label on a can of soup, a dictionary definition of a word, the instructions in a manual, or an advertisement in a magazine. All of these statistics can be taken in a straight way or they can be played with. To play does not just mean to do something funny. A serious poem can emerge from found poetry, such as the following excerpt from David Antin's "Delusions of the Insane," which was derived from an abnormal psychology textbook (published in *Code of Flag Behavior,* Black Sparrow Press, Los Angeles)*:

> a list of the delusions of the insane
> what they are afraid of
>
> the police
> being poisoned
> being killed
> being alone
> being attacked at night
> being poor
> being followed at night
> being lost in a crowd
> being dead
> having no stomach
> having no insides
> having a bone in the throat
> losing money
> being unfit to live . . .

Some of Ronald Gross' *Pop Poems* (Simon and Schuster) are more in the antic vein.**

* Reprinted with the permission of David Antin, copyright © 1968.
** Reprinted with the permission of Simon & Schuster, Inc., New York, copyright © 1967.

NOW IT'S PEPSI

Now it's Pepsi—
   for those who
      think young.

Now
   parties are more
      informal, more fun.

They reflect the new
   way of life
      everyone's leading.

It's called
   thinking
      young.

This is the
   life
      for Pepsi—

light, bracing,
   clean-
      tasting Pepsi.

So think young.
   Say "Pepsi,
      please."

Victor and I tried to create a series of poetry games based on some of the ideas in concrete and found poetry as well as our perception of how many names young people can read and write.

We set simple rules for our first effort. A poem was to be written using the names of people and no other words. The names could be repeated any number of times, modified and placed in any way imaginable on the paper. Instead of trying the name–poetry game with our students we did it first ourselves. (I do myself what I ask others to do. It is cruel to expect students to attempt poetry or art of any sort and not attempt the uncertain, painful work oneself.)

The first time we tried to write minimal poetry we were unsuccessful. We came up with some inane love poems:

> NellyNellyNellyJohn
> NellyBob
> NellySamJamesThomas
> NellNellNellyyyyyyyyyyyy

The creation of minimal poetry seemed a hopeless venture. Fortunately we didn't quit and tried to write minimal poems more than once. Things began to develop and possibilities opened up. One of the teachers we were working with came up with a James Brown poem:

> James
> James Brown
> Brown
> James Brown
> JamesBrownBrownBrown
> BrownJamesBrown

Another used different forms of the same names:

> Robert Bobby Bob
> Richard Dick
> HubertHubertHubert

One of the teachers used elements of concrete poetry to build a picture poem:

```
                    b
                    o
                    b
                    b              l    r
    bobbybobbybobbybobby        g        i   a
                    b                o
                    b
                    o
                    b
```

After our first experiment we expanded the elements in
our minimal poetry. To names of people we added names
of products, then found bits of writing (signs, phrases
from books, advertisements, movie titles, etc.). Finally we
began to add other words such as "no," "if," "but" . . .

One of my students did a minimal poem using "not,"
"but," and product names that went as follows:

> not Pepsi
> not Coke
>   not Buick
>   not Ford
>   not Joy
>   not Mr. Clean
>   but Life Savers
>   LIFE SAVERS

The elements that can be added to minimal poems are
practically unlimited and the complexity of the poems that
can be created is equally unlimited. However, the main
advantage of minimal verse is that it starts where the
learner is and can grow organically.

Words Asked for by the Students

There are some words that beginning readers cannot

recognize in print yet have significance for them and will easily be learned by sight because of their value in people's lives. "Kill," "welfare," "love," "Vietnam," "bomb" are just some examples. These words vary from person to person and culture to culture. Sylvia Ashton-Warner in *Teacher* described how she helped Maori children learn how to read by asking them words they cared about and then writing them down and giving them to the students. Her book is invaluable and her methods can be transposed and modified for almost any setting. Getting words from learners and giving them back in printed form is one way to build up an informal vocabulary that can then be utilized in the ways I mentioned above. It also tells the teacher what interests the learner and is an opportunity to gather the information needed to build a program for learning.

Words Given by the Teacher

There are some words that might not be known in written form by students nor asked for by them, but which embody socially and politically charged aspects of students' lives and which are known to them through their experience.

Racism	Junk
Oppression	Power
Exploitation	Greed
Community	Freedom
Liberation	Destruction
Sexism	Helplessness

are issues in all of our lives. These words have an impact especially on the lives of older beginning readers and can be offered to them not merely to get them to learn to read but to provide the opportunity for them to analyze the conditions of their own lives. It is possible that through the development of control over language, people can come to understand their own capacity to free themselves. The twelve words I listed (there are many more) contain all the letters in the alphabet except Q, V, Z and most of the sound combinations. A study of their meaning can lead to an awareness of one's own personal condition and to the development of a program for change. An analysis of the ways in which the words can be transformed by the learner can lead to the development of the learner's control over language and ability to express his or her own vision of the world. Consider the following transformations:

helplessness ⇢ helpless ⇢ help
powerlessness ⇢ powerless ⇢ power
power ⇢ pow ⇢ plow
sow ⇢ now

Turning "helplessness" into "help" or "powerlessness" into "power" need not be merely a linguistic exercise. If one can use the language to analyze one's own life and express needs and demands, the process of liberation can begin. A discussion of these transformations can lead beyond the words themselves to the political and social realities of the learner's life.

Try your hand at developing and discussing the following transformations:

race ⇢ face ⇢ mace
oppression ⇢ suppression ⇢
destruction ⇢

Paolo Freire is the first person to have talked about using the acquisition of literacy as a vehicle to enable people to become aware of the ways in which they can invalidate the voice and power of their oppressors while achieving their own voice. Freire and his colleagues selected seventeen charged words in Portuguese for each group they assisted with reading. The list of words varied according to the customs and conditions of the people learning to read. These words expressed the conditions of oppression of the Brazilian peasant and contained as well all the syllables necessary to master written Portuguese. Learning to read, learning to be aware of oppression, and freeing oneself are all part of the literacy process Freire uses.

Of course one can object that Portuguese is more regularly syllabic than English, but that is underestimating the power and intelligence of the learner. Once a person has a grasp of many basic regularities of written English, has confidence in him or herself as a learner, and has someone willing to help them, the exceptions to the general forms of our written code provide only a minor problem. Not every sound in the language has to be learned formally. Once the learner understands the ways in which letters represent sounds in our language code, self-teaching is not much of a problem.

As a final note in this section, I have seen the sort of teaching Freire describes done very effectively by some black people in Harlem. In teaching people to read, two of the words used were history and justice. History was broken down to his—story, the white man's way of writing history to serve his own purposes. Then it was varied:

herstory
our story

black story/white story
no more stories
nostory

Similarily justice was looked at as saying:

just us, the courts existing for the white man, or
just ice, the white man's attempt to freeze out black
people, and then transformed: just us →

US black people →
US just →
trust us just people.

Once the learner knows that language can be played
with and can develop transformations and sees his or her
own voice embodied in print, the major obstacle to learning to read, that is fear that one is not capable of learning,
is removed.

3. Words That Connect and Words That Place

There are some words that one cannot afford to sound
out or puzzle over every time they are encountered even
on a beginning level. These words are some of the most
common ones in the language and serve (1) to connect
or modify words or sentences in order to build more complicated forms of expression; (2) to place action, events,
objects, or people in space and time; (3) to tell how
many things, or to indicate whether a specific or general
reference is being made; (4) to indicate the person talking,
spoken about, or spoken to; and (5) to indicate that some
basic form of action or existence is being referred to.

Here is my list of the most basic of these words that

beginning readers must be able to recognize without effort.*

1. connecting and modifying words:
   and   no/not   or   if (if-then)   but   so

2. words that place in time and space:
   when?   now   then
            before   after
   where?   here   there   /   in   out   /   on   off
             to   from   /   above   below

3. words telling how many and how specific and for whom:
   a   the   for   of   some   many   none

4. words referring to people or things:
   I   me   us   we   you   he   she
        it   him   her   them   they

5. some basic words of action and their standard uses:
   is—I am   we are
       you are
       he is   they are
       she is
       it is
       and similarly:
       make, makes, do, does

---

* Other more detailed lists can be made, and lists of this sort should be made and changed according to words most frequently used in people's vocabulary and in the specific written material one is trying to master. Just as my breakdown of reading into four levels emerged from my experience and can be modified if other people perceive other needs, the same is true of my list of basic words to be known from memory. All lists of this sort should be understood as based on the judgment and experience of the teacher and not be considered holy or scientifically necessary. The basic words in my judgment are those that enable the learner to master connections between words and between thoughts. What is crucial is that the learner develop a solid basis on which to teach him or herself, and not that he or she master any particular list.

Altogether there are only forty-seven words on my list, which admittedly is minimal. Learning forty-seven words is no great feat and these words provide one with great power. One way to find out whether people know these words is to ask them. However, if you use flash cards with these words written on them you might get inaccurate information. Usually these words do not appear in the written language by themselves and some of these words (such as "a" and "the") never do. It makes more sense to think up a few interesting sentences, perhaps illustrate them, and ask the learner to read them while you attend to the basic words. Some sentences might be:

The teacher is a kid.
The beer is cold.
She is on 106 Street.

The list of basic words together with an informal vocabulary of about one hundred words provides a good basis for the beginning reader to explore more complex forms of the written word. For example, it is possible to create stories and sentences and poems using the list of forty-seven words plus a list of names, products, song titles, nicknames, etc.

In La Casa de la Raza the teachers in the primary school have started to teach reading to some of the three-, four-, and five-year-olds by posting:

or   and   if   no   not   but

in large print and having the students cut and draw pictures to represent other words.

There are other games that can be played with the basic list of words plus a list of informal words; for ex-

ample, it is possible to put a small list of five basic words
on a blackboard and go around the room asking each
person to contribute the first word that comes to his or her
mind. Then these words can also be transcribed on the
board and everyone in the room be asked to create a poem,
story, or statement using only the small written "uni-verse"
that is written on the blackboard. I have played this game
often, in fact used it daily as a substitute for drill, in order
to get some students of mine to develop an ease and
fluency with the basic words while playing creatively with
language. The game doesn't become too boring since each
day new words are produced by the people playing. After
the first session there is no need for a teacher since the
game can easily be played by a group of people all of
whom are learning to read. The exercise of putting some
of the informally generated words on the board gives the
learners the opportunity to guess at ways of transcribing
their spoken language and to get accustomed to helping
each other and learning collectively without a teacher.

Here is an example of part of a session with high school
students:

basic words:	of	for	no	not
	and	is	on	from	or
	the	a	some

The language universe for the game

words generated by the students:

dope	high
love	never
bed	violet
head	red

Some samples of the writing, which were all read aloud
and discussed and joked about by the group:

a)   some dope   a dope   the dope—
           high   never
           never   high

b)   a red violet bed high
           head high
        so head high
        no high head
        no never
              high head
              never love

c)   a high dope
           from a red bed
        never a love or
              violet head

These are not great poems; the limitation of vocabulary in the game can easily become frustrating. Of course that is the idea. If the game becomes frustrating it is because the language has so many more possibilities, and as students develop some ease and confidence they want access to more complicated thoughts and feelings and ideas. Encourage them to change the rules—do it yourself. Abandon the game when it seems appropriate or make up some new one.

The other day I played the game with students, teachers, and parents from La Casa de la Raza and the following words and phrases generated:

Tequila	Tremendous
Purple liquid	High
Upside down	Slash-flake
Nixon	Chicano
Viva Mexico	*Pato*

Index	Love
McGovern	Zoo
Peace	Marijuana
Face	Magic ball
Try	Catch

It is not surprising that there are some Spanish words included on the list or that some political names appear. The game is open to the concerns and culture of the players. We also changed the rules on the spot to allow phrases because people wanted that complication. Here are the connecting words used and a few sample poems:

it	maybe	a	to
come	no	the	went
with	our	and	if
or	but	not	down
is	I	's	'll

magic catch
with a tremendous magic ball
to the upside down pato zoo school
with down Nixon reading
purple liquid
for marijuana and
high on Viva Mexico
me and
maybe face
love that maybe face

—ISABEL

We love
school
and zoo marijuana
But Pato Nixon:
Down—
catch the magic ball
Upside down—
To Viva Mexico:
Chicano!

—ANDRES

I face
the school the chicano loves
    It's tremendous!
Reading, peace too.
Magic, High
Viva Mexico.
Maybe I'll try.

—ANONYMOUS

Marijuana and tequila is a tremendous high
Peace with love is a purple liquid upside down
Chicano's come . . .
"Viva Mexico," and Nixon down
magic ball catch the face

—PINA

A final game that can be developed with basic vocabulary and some interesting language forms requires getting
hold of some discarded business stamps such as:

Make up some stamps out of words on the basic word list, or let people write those words and use the stamps to develop interesting visual verbal collages.

The stamps themselves also give rise to interesting minimal poems and can be used without the basic words. A whole series of inexpensive stamp sets can be added to the business stamps to make a literacy kit that is fun to use.

4. Alphabet

It is customary to begin discussions of reading with consideration of the alphabet and originally I had considered doing the same. However, in our culture, people are exposed to written words before they are exposed to the alphabet as a particular subject of their attention. Children see words all around them and learn to recognize some of them at an age at which it would make no sense to talk about the alphabet. Their first impression of printed language is probably of words rather than of letters. My daughter Antonia could recognize EXIT before she knew anything about E's, X's, I's, and T's. This phenomenon indicated to me how different the natural process of learning to master a skill can be from the way it is looked at on the basis of an abstract intellectual reduction to so-called basic elements.

From a reductionist point of view, knowledge of the letters should be the first step in learning to read. Then should come the ability to know the sounds the letters represent (or perhaps these things should develop together), and then as a next step words should be recognized. However one can go a long way toward reading in our system without ever encountering a Z.

People learn to recognize letters, name them, and know some of the sounds they represent in varying ways depending on visual preferences, exposure, and probably many other factors we know very little about. For example, most kids learn the letters in their own names much more easily than other letters and some can recognize and even write their names though they do not know many other letters or words. The forms of some letters such as A, E, I, O stand out as unique and are easy to remember. Other letters such as b, p, q, d are easily confused and sometimes it takes more effort to keep them distinct in one's mind. It is not necessary to tell every student all the letters. Discovering in advance how many letters people know simplifies the work. There are two things that should be kept separate: (1) knowing all of the letters in our alphabet either by name or through some of the sounds they represent, and (2) knowing the conventional order of the letters in the alphabet. This latter is not necessary in terms of learning how to read, though it is of great use for anyone who will want to use a dictionary, telephone book, the index of a book, or any other things sorted and organized by letter.

I have used two checklists to find out whether people know the letters:

L K J H G F D S A Q W E R T Y U I O P M N B V C X Z

e i j o s k l p z m b x q r t a v x o d f g h n u y

For people who are too threatened to answer directly about the individual letters, it is possible to devise games using small wooden blocks with letters on them. Naming games can be used: all the letters are put into a big hat, then pulled out one at a time. The first person who names a letter keeps it. At the end of the game, the number of letters each person has is tallied. For young kids the game can be used to familiarize the students with the letters as well as find out what they don't know. As a teacher one needs just to observe as the game is played.

Several sets of the same letters can be used to find out whether a person knows the order of the alphabet if he or she does not want to or cannot recite it. Have each person mix up the letters and then try to put them in a line approximating alphabetical order as best he or she can. The task can easily be turned into a game.

For people who don't know the alphabet it helps to give them a crib sheet which they can use to help themselves. A three-by-five card with the capital and small letters in alphabetical order can be used as well as a series of cards (of the sort used in alphabet lotto games) with the letter and a picture representing an object whose name begins with the letter. Sometimes an attractive poster with the alphabet and some pictures can be put up in the learner's bedroom or kitchen and used whenever necessary. It is up to teacher and learner to discover what works best with that particular learner and use it.

5. Sounds and Combinations of Sounds

There is a lot of talk about phonics in the professional literature on reading. Phonics is considered to present a serious problem to the learner in our language because of the variety of sounds a given letter can represent as well as the variety of letters and combinations of letters that can represent a simple sound. Caleb Gattegno, in *Towards a Visual Culture,* published a black-and-white version of his color-coded chart that gives an indication of the total situation in the English writing system (*see facing page*).

Each column represents a sound that exists in spoken English, and the entries in the column indicate the different ways that sound can be written. If our way of writing were more rational each column would be represented by a single symbol and then we wouldn't have to worry about exceptions and complicated rules. However, the system of writing developed, as did our society and culture, through the mixing of peoples and languages and so for the moment we have to deal with a mulatto form of recording speech and communicating in written form.

There is one thing however that Gattegno's chart points out. First of all, that the situation though complex is finite. There are only a limited number of combinations that exist and these can be mastered. There are fewer than three hundred entries in the chart, and many of them are so close that the number of distinct variations can be reduced to closer to 150. Mastering 150 variations is not much of a problem, especially considering that there are only forty-seven sounds they represent. A friend of mine just returned from China where she observed a number of elementary schools. She said that in the People's Republic of China

Left section (vowel sounds and their spellings):

oi	o								
oi	oy								
ee	ea	e	ie						
oo	ou	u	ew	ui	o				
o	oo	oe	ough	ou	u	ue	ui	ew	wo
a	ai	hei	ea	e	et	ayo			
ou	hou	ow	ough						
o	oe	ow	owe	oa	oh	ew	ou	eau	ough
e	ee	ea	ei	ie	i	eo	oe	ay	ey
u	you	eau	ue	ew	eu	eue	ieu		
a	ay	ey	eigh	aigh	ei	ea	ai		
o	a	au	aw	augh	ough	ou	oo	hau	oa
a	aa	ea	e	ah	au				
i	y	i	igh	ie	eye	ye	eigh	is	ais
a	e	u	o	i	ea	ou	y	ei	ai	ough	ie	iou	io
o	oh	ho	ow	au	ou	a			
e	ie	ea	ai	u	a				
i	y	ey	u	o	ie	ia	a	ay	e	ai	ei	ui
u	o	oe	ou	oo					
a									

Right section (consonant sounds and their spellings):

x	x									
x	x									
x	xe	xc	cc							
qu										
j	g	d	dge	ge	gg	dg	dj			
ch	ng	n								
ch	tch	t	t	c						
sh	ch	t	s	ce	che	ss	sch	sc	ci	
g	gg	gu	gh	gue						
h	wh									
b	bb	be	bu							
r	rr	re	rre	wr	rh	lo	rrh	rt		
k	kk	ke	ck	ch	c	lk	qu	que	cch	che	cc
w	wh	o	u							
th	the									
th	the									
l	ll	le								
d	dd	de	ed	ld						
f	v	ve	lve	ed						
f	ff	fe	ph	lf	gh	u				
n	nn	ne	kn	dne	pn	gn				
m	mm	me	mb	gm	mn	lm				
s	z	ge								
s	ss	se	's	c	ce	sw	st	sc	sch	ps
s	ss	se	z	zz	si	thes	x	's	sch	
t	tt	te	ed	cht	ct	bt	pt	tte	th	
p	pp	pe	ph	ps						

children are not considered ready to learn to read until they are seven or eight, and that by the time they are twelve they have mastered 1,500 written signs or enough to read a newspaper.

There is another important fact about our system of writing. There are major regularities within the system. It is possible to master these regularities without much effort, and to understand that when an irregularity is encountered there are ways to deal with it (like asking someone or using a chart such as Gattegno's).

In order to master most of the phonic regularities of the language it helps to think of syllables (that is, combinations of sounds that make up words) instead of isolated sounds. The so-called vowels a, e, i, o, u (and occasionally y) do not occur in isolation * but are joined with other letters to make sound groups or words, and it is more convenient to study them that way. One way of beginning is to start with a list of words generated by the students and begin to modify them. Such a list might be:

	kill	love	nation
which can be transformed to	will spill fill	dove but not stove which brings up an exception	station situation

Beginning with most any list of words students can learn to make transpositions, to change letters, reverse letters, keep one element constant and vary the others. Some basic

*Except for the words "I" and "A."

sounds can be learned with the alphabet, others learned
by studying the list of informal or generated words. What
is essential is that the learner understand:

1. letters represent sounds;
2. combinations of letters represent a combination of
sounds [what Gattegno elegantly describes as a transformation of the temporal (speech) into the spatial (writing)];
3. varying parts of words by substituting letters vary the
sounds;
4. most of the variations are regular and predictable;
5. exceptions can be dealt with by asking someone who
knows, or thinking of one's own spoken language;
6. words can be created by the learner using these principles.

These six conditions imply that the learner has a sense
of him or herself as learner and can go about teaching himself. For me that is the key to the acquisition of the skill of
reading—the amount of material the teacher needs to convey to the learner is minimal. The gift, the means of
acquiring the skill of reading and many other skills, is in
helping the learner discover how to learn without a
teacher.

Many times when I have tried to describe this method
of helping people master the phonic regularities of English
the first question raised was, What about the silent E?

What about it. The e in "love" is silent, e's at the end of
most words in English act as modifiers and silencers. They
change "mop" to "mope," "cop" to "cope," "pop" to
"Pope." When encountered, the learner can easily deal
with them. And what about "tion" and "au" and "ou" and

the rest of the sound combinations one encounters? All of these things can be taught formally and drilled. Or they can be learned as they are encountered because the learner knows how to ask and has someone to ask; and because teaching oneself is not an alien experience for the learner.

This doesn't mean that the teacher shouldn't prepare— if you want to help others learn how to read, go through all the structured developmental programs you have access to; read Jeanne Chall's *Reading: The Great Debate* to find out what advocates of phonic programs believe. Then use what you have learned in order to give the greatest power and initiative possible to the learner. Share what you know, make it communal property.

A final comment: a beginning reader ought to know as a minimum:

1. the basic sounds associated with the consonants

BCDFGHJKLMN
PQRSTVWXZ

2. The syllables combining these sounds with A, E, I, O, U (Y). Try it yourself by making lists of all the consonants and then adding one vowel at a time before the consonant, then after. For example, start with the vowel a:

ba—   —ab
ca—   —ac
da—   —ad
fa—   —af
ga—   —ag
  "   "
  "   "
  "   "

Then fill in the blanks with different consonants so that you get:

bab	bab
bac	cab
bad	dab
baf	fab
bag	gab
"	"
"	"
"	"

Turn these exercises in list-making into games.

3. How to substitute sounds so that bad → had → glad→dad can be done with ease as well as bad→ bat→ban.

I recently bought a toy manufactured by the Galt company that is useful for practicing substitutions. It consists of three pentagonal-shaped blocks joined together by a wooden peg. Each of the blocks has letters written on all five sides. The middle block has vowels and the end blocks have consonants. The toy looks like this.

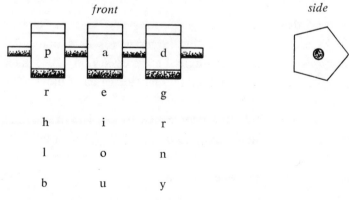

The blocks can be turned so that many three-letter words or sound combinations can be formed. The toy can easily be made and is fun to practice with. For example, starting with "pad," the first block can be turned to give:

rad
had
lad
bad

Similarly the middle block can be turned to give:

pad
ped
pid
pod
pud

For Spanish a fourth block containing the vowels can be added on the end so that the toy would look like this:

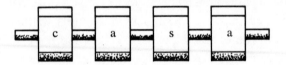

It is also possible to make longer strings of lettered blocks and play with putting larger words or sound combinations together. (It might be necessary in the longer strings to leave a blank face on one side of each block. Try to figure out why.)

Another device some people like to use is a traditional phonic wheel which is easy to make and use for practicing. Here is a sample you can easily make out of paper. It consists of two circles, one small and one large, joined at the

center by a clip so that the circles can be turned around
the center to change the words.

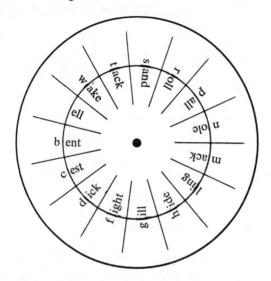

Put together other sounds or words on the inner and
outer wheels. Make up some yourself. Ask your students
to make them.

6. Simple Sentences

Beginning readers should be able to read short sentences
with familiar words as wholes, and not as disjointed collections of words. It is important for students to understand
that sentences have rhythm and that words in the context of
a sentence are modified by each other. The written word
should be referred to the rhythm and movement of the
spoken word in the student's mind. The sentences in Dick
and Jane readers are flat because no one would ever say
them—they are manufactured to appear in basal readers

and have no relationship to spoken language. Therefore, one hears many students brought up on Dick and Jane reading out loud in unnatural stiff voices that are difficult to follow. The sentence

> THE BOY HAD A BALL

can be read as:

> THE / BOY / HAD / A / BALL

or as

> THE BOY / HAD A BALL

or as

> THE BOY / HAD / A BALL

The first reading is stiff and formal. Each word is spoken (or read) as an isolated unit and the sentence has no character. With longer sentences disjointed reading like this confuses the meaning of the whole sentence. For example, try to follow this sentence reading each word separately and pausing between words:

> The boy, who was a bit troubled anyway,
> found himself in a trap and panicked.

The second reading of "the boy had a ball" is probably the most common, putting "the boy" together with "had a ball," indicating possession. The third meaning with its emphasis on "had/a ball" uses the word "ball" to mean a fine time and this is all expressed by the rhythm and intonation with which the sentence is read or spoken.

From the start it is crucial to join the study of sentences

to the study of voice and rhythm. In my beginning reading class (the students were between six and ten) a few years ago the only books available were the Dick and Jane books. Instead of throwing them out we decided to parody them by using different voices to read the stories out loud. For example the sentences

THIS IS DICK
THIS IS JANE
THIS IS SPOT
SPOT IS A DOG

were read in angry, laughing, mocking, sexy, drunken, aged, or babylike voices. Students took turns reading the sentences and varying the rhythm and tone. Then they made up their own stories and varied them in the same way. There was no problem getting even the youngest students to understand that written words expressed voices that could be discovered and played with. Reading when it is just considered a matter of mastering some mechanical skills becomes a dry and often boring activity. When it relates to the voice of the reader or to other people's voices it becomes communication.

NOTE: There is no need to wait to study sentences to introduce voice and tone. Make a list of words, and read them in as many different attitudes as you and the students can imagine.

For example, make a list of words and then suggest students read it in angry, drunken, humorous, bored voice. Do it yourself.

In order to pick out sentences from a text students must

know that sentences are usually marked off by (1) a capital letter for the first letter of the first word of the sentence (and not for the rest of the words) * and (2) a period at the end of the sentence.

Pick up a book or magazine and let the students see for themselves how sentences are marked out. These two pieces of information are not hard to learn though students will quickly pick up the fact that newspaper headlines, captions under photos, and billboards frequently do not observe these conventions. Nor do many contemporary works that are trying to create new language forms.

Sentences in the written language tend to be more completed than in spoken form. When people are physically present and talking to each other they usually have a common context that makes it possible for them to abbreviate continually. For example, if two people were talking about another person, "at the park" is a natural way to indicate where the person is. In written form, "she is at the park" conveys the same information.

A contemporary writer might deliberately use the phrase "at the park" to set a scene and begin a story:

> At the park   She wandered
> about, lost, lonely, frightened.

A writer can choose not to follow the usual forms of the written language. So can anyone. However it is important for people to know the forms they choose to reject. On the level of being able to read and write simple sentences students should know that they generally express complete thoughts and make connections explicit. These completed sentences, which are structured according to the general

---

* With the exception of names and titles, of course.

laws of combining words in our language, are the ones school people call grammatically correct sentences. Thus,

<blockquote>not possible</blockquote>

is not a grammatically complete sentence nor is its meaning explicit when written. For example,

<blockquote>It is not possible.
She is not possible.</blockquote>

are two completions. Teachers are frequently obsessed with completeness and drill into students' heads the need for every sentence to have a subject and a predicate, to have all the articles included, to make sure all the connections implied in the sentence are made clear. Explicitness and completeness are virtues in many cases and students should be aware of the usual ways words in our language function. But they are not moral values and people are not "bad" if they choose to reject them at times.

Some exercises playing with the notion of completeness can be interesting. Take a short sentence—John had a ball—and rearrange it continuously and attempt to make sense out of the different arrangements:

<blockquote>had John a ball
ball John a had
John a ball had</blockquote>

Then leave out a word:

<blockquote>John had ball
had a ball
John had a</blockquote>

Games of this sort give students the opportunity to get a feel for the way language is structured and replace the need for the dull drill that is characteristic of many traditional teaching systems.*

HERE IS A LIST OF BOOKS
ON THE BEGINNING LEVEL

For Younger Learners:

ABC: An Alphabet Book, Platt and Munk, 1966.
Keats, Ezra Jack, *Goggles,* Collier, 1969.
Lewis, Richard, ed., *Miracles,* Simon & Schuster, 1966.
Lewis, Richard, *The Park,* Simon & Schuster, 1968.
Raskin, Ellen, *Nothing Ever Happens on My Block,* Atheneum, 1970.
Sendak, Maurice, *Chicken Soup with Rice,* Scholastic Books, 1968.
Sendak, Maurice, *Where the Wild Things Are,* Scholastic Book Services, 1970.

For Older Learners:

Hughes, Langston, *Black Misery,* Eriksson, 1969.
Laing, R. D., *Knots,* Pantheon, 1970.
Lewis, Richard, comp., *The Way of Silence: The Prose and Poetry of Basho,* Dial, 1970.

---

* Missing from this treatment of sentences and of learning to read in general is an explicit statement about the syntactic and transformational structure of the American language. Noam Chomsky and others have done much work on these forms. However I am concerned with learning more than with analysis in this book, and feel that a mastery of the ability to read can develop without explicit knowledge of the structure of the whole language system. What is necessary is the ability to use the system, which is quite different than knowing about the structure of the system. The same holds true of course for children who learn to talk without explicit articulated knowledge of the rules of the language system.

LEVEL 2: NOT BAD

Levels	Skills
Beginning	
Not Bad	1. Combinations of sounds 2. Complicated words 3. Complex sentences 4. Everyday reading 5. Paragraphs and stories
With Ease	
Complex	

Once one passes beyond the beginning reading level the learner should become increasingly independent and the teacher more of a resource. Many people who have mastered the begining level can teach themselves all they need to know if they become interested in reading books on a particular topic. The crucial thing for the not bad reader is reading experience. At this stage the power to understand unfamiliar material without any assistance begins to develop.

As a minimum, not bad readers should be able to handle

menus, cookbooks, most "how to" manuals, comic books, simple novels and biographies (especially those specifically written for young people and teen-agers), advertisements, and many magazines and newspapers (though *The New York Times* and *Time* and *Newsweek* are probably still beyond them). They should be able to sound out most words they have heard spoken and guess at some that are totally unfamiliar. Stories and articles and other completed forms should begin to be familiar and most of the mechanics of reading mastered. At this level the reader should know:

1. combinations of sounds
2. complicated words
3. complex sentences (including punctuation)
4. advertisements and the media
5. paragraphs and stories

1. Combinations of Sounds

There are some blends of sounds (such as "ph" for "f" sound) that the student might not have encountered frequently as a beginning reader and therefore might not have mastered. An interesting example of a letter combination that might not have been mastered is the "oo" combination, which can be sounded in two different ways:

oo   as in cook, hook, book, crook, etc.
oo   as in food, boot, spoon, choose, etc.

Here reading experience and intelligent guessing are the best aids. Learners need to think about possible meanings and make guesses since there are no automatic formulas by which they could know that the "oo" in "food" has a different sound than the "oo" in "cook."

Most blends of consonant or combinations of consonant letters are easy to master and will be acquired on the beginning level. S-t, t-r, l-k, p-l, etc., provide no trouble. Vowel combinations are more difficult. All the possible combinations of two vowels in English are:

aa	ae	ea	ia	ua
ee	ai	ei	ie	ue
ii	ao	eo	io	ui
oo	au	eu	iu	uo
uu				

Adding a third vowel gives:

aaa	aea	aia	. . .
aae	aee	aii	
aai	aei	aie	
aao	aeo	aio	
aau	aeu	aiu	

The reader can complete the series. The list is finite and many of the combinations never or rarely occur in English. Some of the combinations represent more than one sound. A good exercise for the prospective reading teacher would be to make lists of the various uses of these letter combinations. It might even be possible to help one's students make a phonic dictionary that could be available when no reader was around to ask. For example, each entry could be a vowel combination with a list of words for each sound represented and a few pictures to give the learner a hint.

It would be possible to find a commercially manufactured dictionary of sounds, but it is probably better for learners to make their own and modify it according to their own needs. My guess is that for many learners it will be unnecessary. For others it will hold a great fascination and be referred to even when it is no longer needed as a crutch. For someone who wants to assist others the act of creating a sound book will help provide an intimate familiarity with the peculiar ways our written code works and, therefore, with the knowledge of the kinds of mistakes and confusions that can develop.

Of course there is another way to go about dealing with these phonic issues. Get hold of a structured phonic reading program, or of a series of workbooks, and instead of using them in sequence, give them to students whenever needed in whatever order the needs arise. Learn how to use the material for the learners' purposes.

2. Complicated Words

There are two aspects to complicated words: (1) words that are combinations of many syllables and (2) words whose meanings are unfamiliar. On the not bad level the reader should be able to make an intelligent guess at the sound of almost any word. With the basic knowledge about syllables already acquired on the beginning level, there are a number of ways the learner can build up the habit of reading longer words:

1. The learner should read a lot. It is important to shower learners with printed material on any subject, and let them explore the unfamiliar, guess at words and meanings. Encourage them to be bold enough to make many

mistakes and learn how to correct themselves. At this point in mastering the skill of reading a grading system can devastate the learner. It is as if the child who has just learned to take a few steps were punished for falling. To walk well the child must be bold enough to risk falling and not take it too seriously. The same is true for the fledgling readers: they must be encouraged to take chances, make guesses, figure things out for themselves, ask questions, and become friendly with the printed word.

2. Nonsense syllable games help build up an ability to read longer words easily. For example, here is a list of nonsense words.

inmar   willoway
robororo   millpasser

Pronounce them, make up meanings for them, use them in sentences.

A variant would be to list some syllables:

ir   ick   un
ark   ir   ine

and some letters:

l   v   m   n
r   t   s   b

Combine the syllables and letters to make:

nasty sounding words
sweet sounding words
silly sounding words
angry sounding words
filthy sounding words

Another game I have used with both beginning and not bad readers (as well as with some college students who read quite well) was inspired by Nancy Caldwell Sorel's book *Word People* (American Heritage Press, 1970). The book is a dictionary of words whose origins were in actual people's names. For example some of the entries in the book are:

chauvinism	from Nicolas Chauvin
nicotine	from Jean Nicot
watt	from James Watt
teddy bear	from Theodore Roosevelt

The game consists of taking the names of the people in a group, turning them into nouns, and then creating a meaning for them that relates to the character of the person involved. For example:

from "James" to "a james," meaning
  a pest
from "Willard" to "a willard," meaning
  a long boring journey

Then the created nouns can be added to, varied, used to create new words in the following way:

jamesish	jameslikesion
jameslike	antijamesian
unjameslike	. . .

Introducing prefixes like:

un——	pro——	pre——
anti——	con——	post——

and suffixes like:

———ment   ———wise
———like   ———ish

add to the game as well as to the knowledge of the players.

3. A third way of learning to deal with longer words consists of beginning with compound words (i.e. words made out of two other words such as "underground" and "outside") and playing with modifying them and creating new words. For example:

underground	understand
overground	overstand
middleground	neverstand
playground	newsstand
sleepground	. . .
warground	

The more experience the student has playing with words, creating new forms and juxtapositions, breaking down and building up words and sentences and ideas, the more natural reading and writing will seem, the less threatening, and therefore the easier to master.

So far I have mentioned ways of building the ability to sound words. The other component of complicated words is the ability to guess at meanings of unfamiliar words or to look them up in a dictionary. In my experience, almost all the students considered a dictionary a valuable possession. If possible every student should have one and be shown how to use it. There are different ways to do this. One method is to show one or two learners how to use the book and give them the responsibility for showing the others. Or they can explore the books together and discover how to use them collectively. Finally, a whole group can be given a talk or written instructions on how to use dictionaries. This last method is least satisfactory from my perspective but the context of learning should determine the method chosen rather than any abstract formula.

Prefixes and suffixes like those mentioned above are also useful to puzzle out meaning. The best source for selecting prefixes, suffixes, and roots of words to present to learners is Eric Partridge's dictionary of word origins entitled *Origins* (Macmillan).

There are also games that can point attention to intelligent guessing. For example, create sentences with one nonsense word whose meaning should be obvious from the context and see if the meaning can be guessed.

> He had to *bropbi* or be run over.
> He got hit and ended up with a *xi* eye.
> She closed her eyes and *moplix* him.

Several meanings can be imagined for the word *moplix* in the third sentence, but that makes the game more interesting.

3. Complex Sentences

Starting with a simple, not particularly interesting sentence like

(1) John is a boy

there are an infinite number of ways to build up more complex, interesting expressions. Let me experiment with one way:

(2) John is a strange boy.

(3) John, though he seems nice, is a strange boy.

(4) John, though he usually seems nice, is a strange boy.

(5) John, though he usually seems nice, is a strange unhappy boy.

(6) John, though he usually seems nice, is a strange unhappy boy who sees weird monsters and hears threatening voices.

Sentence (1) is transformed to sentence (2) through adding the word "strange," which gives more information about John and at the same time raises the question of how he is strange. Modifying words can be played with, especially once the reading of simple sentences is no problem. "A strange boy" can be changed to "a simple boy," "a black boy," "a stupid boy" or added to "a very strange boy," "a silly and strange boy," "a strange sick boy."

On the not bad level students should be able to modify sentences by adding descriptive and qualifying words, to read sentences that have such strings of descriptions, and to write them too.

It is fun to make a further modification of sentence (2) to read:

(7) John is as strange as a loon

and play with the notion of comparisons, which should provide no problem on the not bad level. For example:

he's as ugly as a————

can lead to all kinds of interesting comparisons:

                              witch.
         ugly as a————baby.
                              pig.
                              fat man at the circus.
                              sleek Cadillac.

I used to play comparison games with my sixth-grade class and used beginning statements such as:

    He's as wild as a————.
    It's as beautiful as a————.
    We're as happy as a————.

These comparison games turned into praising games and insulting games where the blank had to be filled in by a praise or curse. People kept on elaborating on themes and building up unexpected comparisons:

    He's as wild as a mouse.

                    cowardly mouse.

                    cowardly mouse that couldn't beat
                    a flea in a punching contest.

                    cowardly mouse whose whole fam-
                    ily couldn't beat a flea in a punch-
                    ing contest.

In my experience teaching reading I have found that the more learners play with language, modify sentences and descriptions, write crazy things, the easier and more natural reading other people's writing becomes. Instead of teaching formal grammar, which is unnatural and removed from the act of reading and writing, it is possible to play with building up complex sentences, changing them, getting familiar with adding parts that tell more than the simple sentence or change the whole feeling or meaning of the sentence. Thus sentence (2) was built into sentence (3) by adding the series of words "though he seems nice" and marking off the addition by two commas so the reader won't be confused. The use of commas, colons, and semicolons need provide few problems if introduced as ways of keeping parts of sentences and ideas separated in order to avoid confusion as well as to indicate where the author wants the reader to pause.

The words introduced in sentence (3) can also be changed so that (4) "though he *usually* seems nice" results. One can play with introducing and changing phrases. "Though he seems nice" can go through a series of playful transformations:

→ though he used to seem nice →
though he tried to seem nice →
though he wanted to seem nice

Thinking about the meanings of words and phrases and sentences and about the ways they can be combined gives the learner power over language. The easier one feels with words and sentences, the less formidable the task of deciphering unfamiliar texts becomes.

"John, though he usually seems nice, is a strange unhappy boy who sees weird monsters and hears threatening voices" is a complicated sentence yet easy to read if one knows how to go about reading it and has a sense of how it is constructed. This doesn't mean that the reader has to know how to diagram the sentence in a formal manner. Rather the reader has to be able to grasp that the sentence is about John, that his strangeness is being accented and described, and that a few words have been thrown in to fill out the description of the way he usually seems to other people.

The ability to deal with complex sentences develops through reading a lot and through some experience with building and modifying sentences. Writing and reading, the making of one's own sentences and words as well as the understanding of the words of others, can develop simultaneously and support each other. Most of the suggestions for teaching and learning in the book deliberately combine reading and writing though the emphasis is on reading.

There is another fascinating way to explore how language is built out of experience. A few years ago while playing insult and praise games (adopted from some of the work the novelist Mark Mirsky did with John Hawke's Voice Project) with some college students I noticed how naturally we all tended to use animals to describe people. This set us on a quest to discover how many animal phrases we could find in our language. Here is a part of the list of over 2,000 phrases we came up with:

ANIMAL EXPRESSIONS

Ass   silly ass
        asinine
        mulish, muling
        stubborn as a mule
        mulatto

Bat   old bat

bats in the belfry
batty (bats)
blind as a bat

Birds   bird (girl)
rare bird
pigeon (girl)
stool pigeon
pigeon: one who lets himself be swindled
to treat as a pigeon, make a pigeon of
to pluck a pigeon (to fleece a person)
pigeon pair (boy and girl twins)
pigeon-hearted (timid)
pigeon-livered (meek, gentle)
hawk: one who preys on others
hawk: officer of the law who pounces on
  criminals
hawk: effort made to clear one's throat
hawk: carry about from place to place, offer
  for sale
ball hawk
hawk nose
it's for the birds
gullible
to gull
eats like a sparrow (or bird)
bird feed (seed?) i.e. no money
eagle eye
an old crow
cuckoo (crazy)
birdbrained
cock robin

head in sand

as cruel as an ostrich

ostrichism: policy of hiding one's head like
   an ostrich

his feet and legs are like an ostrich

thy stomach is like an ostrich; it can digest
   hard iron

who in the stupid ostrich . . .

wise as an owl

owl eyes

blinks like an owl

as drunk as an owl

to take owl (to be offended)

to fly with the owl (to be out of doors after
   sunset)

owl: downy nonsense

to owl about (moon about out of doors in
   the dark)

night owl

There are many ways to play with this list:

1. Use the phrases in describing things or people.
2. Change the phrases: e.g.
       silly ass to ↛
       smart ass ↛
       wise ass ↛ dumb ass
       birdbrained ↛ hawk brained
       ↛ frog brained ↛
       monkey brained
and then figure out meanings for the changes.
   3. Create new verbs like some of the old ones on the

list. For example, "to gull" exists in our language.
What about:

> to bear   to pigeon
> to cat   to dog

4. Make up lists of expressions in our language that use:

> flowers
> objects
> machines
> the weather

NOTE ON DIAGNOSIS: How you discover which sentences a student can read.

Anyone who tries to help people learn how to read must constantly observe the learner's efforts to teach him or herself without being too obtrusive or pushy. Over a period of time the teacher should know quite specifically what each student can and cannot do. Diagnosis, teaching, and learning are continual and interrelated activities. Learners can come to understand what they don't know, diagnose their own inadequacies, and develop programs for themselves. Or they can ask for help. The teacher can offer help, offer his or her perception of what the learner needs, make suggestions. Ideally the teacher and learner should feel free to criticize each other, to ask questions and make suggestions. The learner should be able to tell the teacher that he or she is wrong or mistaken or pressing too hard or not understanding. The teacher should be equally free to express his or her perceptions. In this situation of dialogue and exchange formal tests are not relevant. The teacher and learner know in specific and individual form what is known, what is needed, and what can be offered.

However, there are some aids to diagnosis. A few months ago Victor Acosta, Carmen Alegria, and I were talking about how one could tell the level of complexity on which students were able to read. I showed them the Gates Diagnostic material and we looked at the story that it used:

1.

The boy had a dog.
The dog's face was black.
The dog's body was brown.

2.

Once the dog saw a rat.
It was a bad rat.
The dog did not like the rat on his place.
So he ran the rat into his hole.

3.

After the rat got into his hole, he began to peek at the dog.
This drove the dog nearly mad.
He said: "I like raw meat to eat. It you do not stop, I will
    eat you."
Then he left the rat alone.

4.

This talk only made the rat smile.
He could not stop smiling.
He stuck out his chin and cried:
"You are as dull as a donkey.
You are as silly as a monkey.
Let me give you a good tip.
You had better find a doctor now,
    before it is too late.
Maybe he can do something for your head."

5.
These remarks made the dog furious. He was
so angry he could hardly control himself. He
growled in dismay. He gnawed at the ground.
Then he barked: "I am the protector of this
residence. I am the champion of this estate.
I will have no nonsense here. If you value
your life and freedom you will depart at once."

The story begins simply and gets increasingly more complex. Somewhere the student with reading problems is
expected to break down and thereby provide information
about his or her problems. We all agreed that the idea
behind the story was good. However, the story itself was
boring; and the language, especially toward the end, was
unnatural. The format was uninteresting. No one I know
would want to read such a text. We decided to make up
a story ourselves, begnning with the simplest sentences
and words and getting more and more complex. We tried
to create a story about kids and a crazy pig, with funny
pictures and an interesting plot.

Most kids who have read the story, including my own,
like it. They are also intrigued by the idea that the writing
gets more and more complex, a fact that we tell them. A
number of youngsters have used the story to test themselves and see where they break down. The story functions
as a diagnostic instrument, a self-teaching device, but
mostly as a story.

Learners and teachers can create their own diagnostic
stories, can experiment with developing more and more
complex sentences. It is probably best for people to make
up stories that relate to the lives and language and culture
and age of their students.

As a final note, I want to mention an unhealthy use of
the pig story. I observed a "professional" teacher sit down
with a young person and ask him to read the book. The
student began, then broke down over the word "furious."
At that point the teacher made a note of the problem,
took the book from the student, and went on to another
student. The student was frustrated—he wanted to hear the
rest of the story and asked if the teacher could read to
him. The request was refused, the teacher informed me,
because the diagnosis was done and there was no need
to go further. The teacher wasn't interested in the student
but in the diagnosis—wasn't interested in what was happening at that moment with that particular reader. Diagnosis as a form of testing replaced the sensitive dialogue
between learner and teacher, which is the essence of the
teaching-learning relationship. The moment was right for
the teacher to read the rest of the story and perhaps even
help the student try again himself.

4. Everyday Reading

There are certain printed materials that people encounter
in their everyday life that they should be able to read on
the not bad level. These materials include: the telephone
book, *TV Guide*, bus and plane schedules, catalogues,
menus, advertisements (especially those which proclaim
SALE), instructions that are included with appliances,
price lists in supermarkets, newspapers, campaign literature, posters, buttons, and "how to" manuals.

Not all of these forms will be equally interesting or
relevant to younger and to older people. For example,
instructions on how to play games or make models will

probably be of greater interest to twelve-year-olds than instructions on assembling a vaccum cleaner or food blender. "How to" manuals will also hold different people, depending upon whether they are interested in repairing cars, sewing, building furniture, learning macramé, etc.

The same obviously holds true of bus schedules and campaign literature, which will probably hold little interest for five- and six-year-olds.

In our culture some printed material does interest or at least distract people of most ages: menus, *TV Guide,* catalogues, food and car ads, labels on packages, etc. In putting together a collection of everyday reading material it is important to get a sense of what the learners' interests are, what their level of sophistication is outside of the context of reading (nine-year-olds and thirty-five-year-olds who read on the same level do not have the same interests or awareness of life), and what is of interest in their culture. For example, "how to" manuals relating to macramé, knitting, and flower gardening would turn off a group of young black teen-age males because of their identification with hippie culture and female stereotyped values. Of course these manuals can be used with some students to break down stereotypes. For example, I taught myself macramé through a do-it-yourself manual and have used my interest in tying knots as a way of getting some teen-age males to overcome their sense that certain crafts are women's stuff and, therefore, to break down some sexual prejudices that exist in our culture.

"How to" manuals, bus schedules, menus, etc., consist of instructions that can be transformed by the reader into action. They take him or her beyond the page itself and involve acting, choosing, or making and repairing things.

The ability to master these materials increases the reader's power over his or her life and, therefore, are highly interesting to beginning readers.

Here are some possible packets of everyday reading materials put together for different learning situations:

A. An all Chicano, bilingual elementary and junior high school
   a. bilingual menus
   b. Mexican cookbooks in Spanish and English
   c. copies of telephone books
   d. TV guides
   e. bus schedules
   f. commercially printed advertising material hustled from local restaurants and stores
   g. collection of posters and buttons put out by La Raza
   h. collection of old tickets to athletic events
   i. minibike repair manuals
   j. "how to" manuals on painting, sculpture music, etc.
   k. plastic models with the directions reproduced for lots of kids
   l. "how to" home repair books
   m. sets of chess, checkers, dominoes with instructions included

This material can be used for reading. It can also be used to provide samples that the students can take off on in writing. For example students can (1) design their own buttons and posters; (2) write ads for imaginary products; (3) put together their own cookbooks or get recipes from their parents and put together a cookbook entitled The Neighborhood Cookbook, or Our Home Cookbook, or La Raza Cookbook; or (4) develop their own repair manuals or instruction booklets for street games they play, etc.

    B. A hip-oriented, predominantly white junior high
        a. natural foods cookbook
        b. backpacking guides
        c. wilderness survival manuals
        d. the boy scout handbook
        e. posters and buttons of a "hip" nature
        f. do-it-yourself manuals on a whole variety of subjects
        g. yoga manuals
        h. massage manuals
        i. underground newspapers

Of course it is foolish to stick to one stereotyped image of the learners' culture. Though most of the materials selected may relate to the learners' perceived interests there is no harm in throwing in materials that might expose them to unfamiliar situations. To the above, for example, can be added (j) a collection of political advertisements ranging from the Birch Society through the Democrats and Republicans to the Progressive Labor and Yippie parties, (k) the Black Panther Newspaper, *Muhammed Speaks,* and (l) the *Daily News.*

The list is practically unlimited and teachers and learners can put together constantly changing collections of materials according to their interests and the resources available to them.

C. A predominantly black, predominantly poor community high school

  a. telephone books
  b. TV guides
  c. "how to" books
  d. posters, buttons
  e. the Blank Panther Newspaper, *Muhammed Speaks*
  f. a gospel song handbook
  g. sheet music
  h. soul cookbook as well as other cookbooks
  i. comparative price lists from different stores
  j. a collection of catalogues
  k. wilderness survival manuals
  l. advertising material from local stores
  m. lists of top records
  n. radio schedules
  o. concert schedules, a set of old tickets to concerts and dances
  p. wedding and party invitations
  q. greeting cards
  r. political handbills
  s. a collection of matchbooks

The list can go on indefinitely and the students can (1) create their own songs; (2) make up party and wedding invitations; (3) develop funny or serious greeting cards; (4) develop their own community newspaper; (5) write ads for shows; (6) study prices in supermarkets throughout the community; and (7) develop catalogues of resources in their community or of imaginary objects.

A collection of everyday reading materials is cheap to

obtain and can constantly be renewed since our society is so wasteful. Back date magazines and newspapers, obsolete ads, material from last year's political campaigns, bus schedules, telephone books, menus, matchbooks can be acquired free and in quantities so that no program however poor need go without printed material.

5. Paragraphs and Stories

On the not bad reading level people should be able to read comic books, simple romances and sport stories, biographies, jokes, tales, fables, and some simple narrative novels. They should have a sense of plot and be able to hold a story or argument together in their minds while reading.

Most people tell tales and jokes, and one natural way to expose people to longer forms of reading and writing may be through their own jokes and tales. A tape recorder comes in handy here though it is not necessary. A way to begin is to ask for jokes and tales—gossip, stories about people's past, rumors. These can be recorded on tape and then transcribed exactly as they were spoken or, if there is no machine, can be written out directly using a minimum of punctuation or paragraphing. Then the written forms can be reread both aloud and silently and worked upon so the reader can follow the line of thought. The material can then be divided in sections that have natural breaks (i.e. the learners can discover paragraphing for themselves); sentences that are too long can be broken down or divided with semicolons or colons. In the attempt to keep a joke intact and at the same time make it readable a great deal can be discovered about the problems of transposing the spoken word into writing.

Another way to get people involved in writing stories and becoming accustomed to reading them is through the use of fables and their morals. Fables can be as simple as:

The Head Man

This guy was born, but he was just a head. So he went to a witch doctor and he said, "I don't want to be just a head." The witch doctor put up his hands and went puff and turned him into a hand.

Then the guy ran around hollering, "I don't want to be a hand!"

There is a moral to this story: "You should have quit while you were a head."

and as sophisticated as:

Birds, Beasts and Bat

Not too long ago one of the higher-ups among the hawks spotted a succulent fish in a stream far below him, and began his dive for it. He had been flying high, for by the time he got there, a bear had the fish hooked on one paw and was about to take a bite out of it. "Get your dumb paws off that fish," screeched the hawk, "it's mine." "You must be kidding," said the bear, and with one swipe of his free paw he broke the hawk's right wing. The hawk limped off through the brush, cursing and screaming. "I'm not gonna forget this—I'll be back with a few of my friends and we'll see how tough you are then, fat stuff!" The hawk gathered his friends, and the bear gathered his friends, and before anybody realized what was happening, a full-scale war between the birds and the beasts had begun. Every creature in the world took sides, except for one.

"I figure it this way," said Bat to himself: "I'll see which side looks like it'll come out on top, and join that one." He knew that with his leathery wings he could easily pass for a bird, and with his ears and claws he could pass for a beast.

Bat made himself a tricky reversible soldier's uniform, with bird insignia on one side and beast insignia on the other. When the beasts looked as if they would wipe out the bird forces, Bat turned his uniform beast-side out and joined them, screaming, "God is on our side" and "liberate the air!" He killed all the tiny birds he could find. When the birds had the upper hand, Bat went home, reversed his uniform, flew back into the fray crying, "God is on our side" and "liberate the land!" He killed all the mice and other little animals he could find.

The war was fierce and bloody, and went on for many months. At last the beasts and birds, tired of fighting and sick of bloodshed, decided to make peace. Both sides wrote and signed many complicated treaties and documents, and set up all kinds of commissions and organizations to make sure there would never be another war. I am sorry to tell you that despite all the promises, there were other wars anyway, as silly as this one and even more horrible. But whether they were at peace or war, from that time on neither side would have Bat.

"You fought for the beasts," screamed the Eagle, King of Birds, "so you must be one. Go live with your friends. And never let us catch you flying in our air again!"

"You were on the side of the birds," roared the Lion, King of All Animals, "so, of course, you are a bird. Go live with them, and never let us catch you on land again!"

After all this Bat became so confused and unhappy that he himself no longer knew if he was bird, beast, or anything at all. From that time until today, rejected by all sides, he has sneaked around at night, and lived in dank caves and old barns. He can fly like a bird, but he never sits in trees, singing in the sunlight. Nobody knows exactly what kind of creature he is, and nobody cares.

Moral: If you try to sit on two chairs at once, you'll end up on the floor between them.

A few years ago Karen Kennery and I compiled a booklet on fable writing for the Teachers and Writers Collaborative * in which we suggested certain ways of going about creating fables. One way for example is to start with a moral or proverb and create stories to fit it. A list we thought up included:

Morals

Anti-Moralizing and Cynical Morals

Don't believe what the teacher says.

If you live as humans do, it will be the end of you.

A deaf audience is better than none at all.

Don't get it right, just get it written.

If someone has been bad to you, give them a taste of their own medicine.

A friend in need is a pain in the neck.

Never believe a relative.

Do unto others as others *do* unto you.

Women are like the sea, which smiles and lures men onto its sparkling surface, then snuffs them out.

If only he had had no friends, he might have reached old age.

Happiness is a First National City Bank!

It is not so easy to fool little girls nowadays as it used to be.

Don't believe your children because they might get you in trouble.

Be Careful, Deliberate

Don't play with fire.

It is better to ask some of the questions than to know all the answers.

* Teachers and Writers Collaborative, Horace Mann-Lincoln Institute Teachers College, Columbia University, New York, N.Y.

He who hesitates is sometimes saved.

Don't eat animals you don't know.

Never trust a dog—friendly or not.

Don't nibble at anyone's cracker but your own.

Don't smile if you don't have teeth.

Never pick on anyone who's bigger than you.

Never flirt with a lady whose husband is a fighter.

Never have too much furniture.

Don't play around with anything of importance.

Don't play games with smart little girls that have guns.

A bird in the hand is worth two in the bush.

Don't put all your eggs in one basket.

Never try to take someone out of a cage or you might get
locked in.

Each man, to save his life, would never take more than
one loving wife.

Don't shine your head too much.

The Truth in Generalities

As a priest is, so is the parish.

Consort with bad men and you will be hated just as they
are, even though you yourself do no injury to those
around you.

As the twig is bent the tree is inclined.

Show me a man's friend and I'll tell you who he is.

All's Hopeless Anyway

There is no safety in numbers, or in anything else.

You may as well fall flat on your face as lean over too far
backward.

The world is like a candy jar. If you try to take a piece
you might get a stomach ache.

Don't bother, or you'll be hurt.

If you are ugly, stay ugly.

Ashes to ashes, and clay to clay, if the enemy doesn't get
    you your own folks may.

Open most heads and you will find nothing shining, not
    even a mind.

Another group of themes people seem to enjoy spinning
tales about have to do with the origins of peoples, places,
things, or habits. Topics such as these are fun to play
with:

> why the camel has a hump
> why people don't eat with their hands
> how the spider got to make a web
> how the cockroach was given the earth
> why there are only two sexes
> why there are even two sexes
> how people learned to laugh
> how people learned to cry

Whatever form of writing the learner attempts it is important for him or her to understand and believe that it is
natural to make mistakes. Most people dread rereading
their own works because school has somehow instilled in
them the idea that writing must be done correctly and
well the first time. Most of my first attempts at expression
are muddled, inconsistent, sketchy, sometimes clumsy. I
look at my first efforts as a base upon which to build a
decently written work. Most professional writers I know
do constant reworking of their material and many feel they
never achieve all they would like to. If learners approached
reading and writing expecting to make mistakes and understanding that dealing with those mistakes is part of the

substance of learning, reading and more especially writing would not seem such a difficult skill.

As the learner has mastered the not bad stage he or she should be able to pick up books and newspapers without much assistance. At this point exposure to the widest range and variety of books is important, as well as discussions (not lectures) about reading.

I have found that collective reading and discussion is one of the most effective ways to assist people in feeling easy with the written word. A group of people reading a story or essay aloud, interrupting each other to discuss points raised in the text, or merely to take off from the text and talk about things on their minds, is an effective way to connect reading with life. Bible study groups or Maoist reading groups have hit on an essential function of the written word—that is to provide a focus from which people can move to explore important areas of their lives. Some of the best reading groups I have been in have sometimes spent hours talking about a single sentence. In a fifth-grade class I taught, the line "Poor Americans are better off than most of the people in the world" led to a long discussion of welfare, comparative poverty, and the nature of textbook writers. At another time a group of high school students and I spent four months reading the first forty pages of R. D. Laing's *The Politics of Experience*. We talked about our own families and lives, about the ways in which madness invaded our lives, about our experiences with drugs. The fact that we did not finish the book was not essential to our purpose, which was to use Laing's work as a vehicle to explore our own lives.

The collective reading group is not the same as the traditional teacher-directed reading out loud of a text. In the traditional context the teacher decides who is to read, how much is to be read, what questions are to be asked, and what the correct answers are. For the collective group someone begins the text. Anyone can interrupt, question, bring up an issue. Equally, anyone can suggest people stop bullshitting and get back to the text. Furthermore the selection of the book is up to the group and if anyone has trouble reading the text out loud it is the group's responsibility to help and support him or her. There is no one sitting in judgment. If someone plays a teaching role (and that is not necessary) that means he or she has some knowledge or experience to add to the group that is not otherwise present. The teaching person is not a judge or executioner but rather someone with a gift to offer that may or may not be accepted.

The following is a list of books I judge to be on a not bad reading level. They range from the simplest to the most sophisticated books that still have the limited vocabulary and fairly uncomplicated structure that I find characteristic at this level. Please remember that this is a matter of my judgment and that anyone is free to make his or her own analysis of the process of reading.

Jordan, June, *His Own Where,* Crowell, 1971.

Jordan, June, *Who Look at Me,* Crowell, 1969.

Jordan, June and Teni Buch, collected by, *The Voice of the Children,* Holt, Rinehart and Winston, 1970.

Lester, Julius, *Black Folktales,* Grove, 1970.

Lester, Julius, *To Be a Slave,* Dial, 1968.

Malo, John W., *Wilderness Canoeing,* Collier, 1971.

Meilach, Dona Z., *Macramé—Creative Design in Knotting,* Crown, 1971.

Nicholas, A. X., ed., *The Poetry of Soul,* Bantam, 1971.

LEVEL 3: READING WITH EASE

Levels	Skills
Beginning	
Not Bad	
With Ease	1. Unfamiliar words 2. Different forms of writing 3. Voice 4. Test taking
Complex	

A person who reads with ease is comfortable with the printed word. There is a point at which the learner stops struggling to figure out the sounds of words or the flow of sentences. At that point he or she ceases to be conscious of being a learner and becomes simply a reader. It is like children learning to speak. At a certain point they no longer need to struggle with words and sounds and sentence forms and begin to speak easily with their own voices. That doesn't mean that they never make mistakes or don't have more to learn about speaking. It is more that the basic structure of the language has been mastered and speaking has become a habit. The same holds true with reading—at a certain point most materials can be read right off without thinking. There will be gaps in the reader's knowledge—words that have never been seen before, sentences that need to be untangled, books whose meanings have to be puzzled out. However the reader will be free to concentrate on these specific gaps in his or her experience with the printed word without having at the same time to worry about every word or sentence. Knowing one can read, it is possible to concentrate on becoming a more skillful and experienced reader.

There are several specific areas of reading people can work on once they have gone beyond the not bad level and begun to read with ease. First is the development of a way of dealing with unfamiliar words. Second is the conscious study of different forms of writing—poetry, fiction, reporting, describing, etc. Third is the study of the voices writers use in their work. Finally there is the matter of test taking—at this point in a person's reading career it makes sense to prepare oneself to deal with the variety of written tests that have to be dealt with in our culture. These four aspects of reading with ease will be dealt with in some detail.

1. Unfamiliar Words

There are two issues here: (1) building up a large vocabulary and (2) developing strategies to deal with words one does not know when they are encountered in print.

Building a large vocabulary need not consist of memorizing lists of unfamiliar words and their meanings. With the aid of a dictionary and a thesaurus * there are a num-

---

* A book that groups together words of similar or opposite meanings. *Roget's College Thesaurus,* The New American Library, New York, 1962.

ber of ways of going about acquiring a powerful vocabulary:

1. Start with a word whose meaning you don't know. Look it up in the dictionary, read the different meanings listed. Then instead of closing the dictionary look above and below the word you started with for related words. Try to find a family of related words and understand the way the meanings vary. Suppose you start with "sophisticated." Listed above the word in the *American Heritage Dictionary* are, going up the column:

sophisticated → sophisticate
→ sophist → sophism → Sophia
→ soph. (abbreviation of sophomore)
→ sop. (abbreviation of soprano)

Going down the column one finds:

sophistry → Sophoclean → Sophocles
→ sophomore → sophomoric → Sophy →
-sophy (as in philosophy) → sopor

The dictionary entries "sop." and "sopor" are not part of the family. The rest are. From the dictionary one learns that the family consists of variations on the Greek word "sophia," which means wisdom but which can also stand for false wisdom (as in sophism).

Uncovering word families and the central word that binds them together gives one a sense of how language grows and how words are created. It also provides the learner with a range of words that would only be naturally encountered over years of serious reading.

2. There are some common Greek and Latin words

(such as "sophia") that provide the core upon which many English words and families of words are built. It is fun to study the actual ways these words are used as well as create new uses for them. An exhaustive list of them can be found in the appendix of *Origins* (Eric Partridge) or in most dictionaries. I'll give only a few:

> *logos*—Greek for "The Word" (as in the Bible, "In the Beginning was the logos, the word")
>> Members of the family:

*log*ical	dia*log*ue	pro*log*ue
*log*ic	mono*log*ue	
*log*istics	trave*log*ue	
log (diary)	physcho*log*y	
*log*arithm	socio*log*y	

> *anima*—Latin for the soul
>> Members of the family:

*anima*l	*anima*te
in*anima*te	*anima*ted cartoon
*animo*sity	*anima*tion
*anim*us	

> *psyche*—Greek for the soul or spirit (in Greek myth a young woman in love with Eros, or Cupid. Eventually they married, uniting body and spirit)
>> Members of the family:

*psych*ology	*psych*ologist
*psych*ic	*psych*edelic
*psych*osomatic	*psych*o
*pysch*oanalysis	*psych*omotor
*psych*osis	

astron—Greek for star
Members of the family:
*astro*nomy   dis*aster*
*astro*naut   *astro*dome
*astro*labe   *astro*logy

Limiting ourselves to the four words *logos, anima, psyche,* and *astron,* let's imagine some ways of creating new words:

astropsyches—the spirits of the stars
loganimal—the language of animals
astronanimalogy—the study of animal life on the stars
animalogy—the study of or word about the soul

Add a few qualifying parts of words like anti (against) or pro (for) and you get:

antianima and proanima
an antiastropsyche
. . .

Playing games with words helps people sharpen their ability to say or write what they intend as well as accustom them to figuring out the writing of others. It is important for readers not merely to understand the dictionary meaning of a word, but to understand how a particular writer in a specific situation uses or changes that meaning.

3. Another way to build up a vocabulary is to pick a simple, descriptive word, vary it by extending or qualifying its meaning, and then discover whether there are words that embody those variations. Let me illustrate what I mean:

Start with the descriptive word "fat." Vary it:

no fat at all
somewhat fat
pleasantly fat
ugly fat
very fat
fat and fleshy
fat and stupid

Then begin with words you know that have the meaning of some of your variations:

no fat at all—lean
somewhat fat—stout
pleasantly fat—chubby

Then using a thesaurus or asking around other words can be introduced:

very fat—obese
fat and fleshy—corpulent
ugly fat—porcine

If you end up with a qualification of the original word that you can't find a word for, make one up:

fat and stupid—fatid
        or stupfat
        or stupig
        or dumbese

Try some yourself. What words in our language are or could be used to mean the following variations of the word "smart"?

smart and understanding———
smart and snobbish———
smart in a deep way———
smart verbally———
smart intellectually but dumb in life———
too smart for him or herself———
smart and sassy———

the word "pretty"?

very pretty———
too pretty———
pretty and dumb———
pretty and intelligent———
deceptively pretty———
pretty in a phony way———
pretty in a shallow way———

4. Another way to discover unfamiliar words is to extend the above exercise to other subjects such as work people do, personality traits, physical descriptions, attitudes and beliefs, etc. For example:

What is the name for someone who
——— fixes toilets
——— repairs cars
——— builds spaceships
——— works on an assembly line
——— sells dope

What do you call someone who
——— is always nasty
——— is always smiling
——— lies all the time

——— is always on the hustle

——— is lazy but smart

——— is full of energy but dumb

What do you call someone who

——— has too many muscles

——— seems to have no muscles

——— stumbles all over him or herself

——— moves with ease and grace

——— responds quickly

——— looks the way nobody else looks

How do you describe a person who

——— only listens to him or herself

——— believes something no matter what anyone else says

——— changes his or her mind all the time

——— is reasonable

——— responds on the basis of feelings and not ideas

——— responds on the basis of ideas and not feelings

A dictionary, a thesaurus, and some friends can help to figure out what characteristics our language singles out and names because they mean something to people in our culture. It is also interesting to discover those aspects of life that don't merit enough attention to be named.

5. There are many other ways to build vocabulary, which are outlined in traditional school textbooks that might be worth looking at. As a final note I recommend *30 Days to a More Powerful Vocabulary,** an inexpensive

* Wilfred Funk and Norman Lewis, published by Funk and Wagnalls.

self-teaching book that is intelligently designed and fun to go through.

At times while reading a book or an article you'll come upon a word you've never seen before. There are several things that can be done to figure out these words. If the meaning of the word is clear from the context it is possible to continue reading with little or no loss of meaning. For example, in the sentence "He has been eating so much recently that he has become quite corpulent and has a hard time getting around," the word "corpulent" clearly means fat.

Often it is not possible to guess merely from a sentence what a key word means. For example, the meaning of the same word "corpulent" cannot be guessed from the following sentence: "A corpulent man entered the room." In case the meaning of a word can't be guessed there is always the dictionary or a friend to ask. If the meaning of the word makes no difference to the meaning of the story the word can be skipped and its meaning never learned.

I am curious about unfamiliar words and like to make notes when reading as well as copy out phrases or sentences I want to remember. I also dislike using a dictionary while reading. Looking up words breaks my concentration on the flow of the text. Therefore I read with a pencil in my hand. If it is possible to get by without looking up an unfamiliar word I jot it down and return to it after reading. Occasionally, of course, I encounter a word whose meaning is so central to what is being read that the dictionary has to be consulted.

2. Different Forms of Writing

Hopefully anyone reading with ease will have encountered many different forms of writing. However it helps at this stage to think about some of the forms themselves rather than merely take them for granted. It is also time to struggle with difficult books and poems and articles.

In school it is customary for teachers or textbooks to define poetry or fiction or narrative journalism in a particular way and give the student the impression that there is a clear line between writing that does or doesn't fit in each category. Thus students are told that poems must rhyme or have certain rhythms or certain spacing on the page. Then examples are provided that fit the definition, and anything that does not fit is considered not a poem. I have seen ridiculous arguments develop over whether some contemporary poems are "really" poems. Certainly a rigid definition will exclude a lot of material. However the more rigid the definition the less use it will be to the reader. The line between poetry and prose, between fiction and nonfiction, is neither clear nor fixed. As new forms of writing develop the line shifts. In a nontrivial way poems are what poets write. People who consider themselves working within the tradition of poetry define and redefine that tradition all the time. It is important to understand that all poems or stories or novels do not have common properties so much as family resemblances. Let me explain what I mean.

Suppose we consider the Brown family—mother, father, and two children—James and Susan. Susan has her father's nose and her mother's eyes. James has his mother's nose and his father's eyes. To look at James and Susan you would never know that they were brother and sister. However, if you knew the whole family you would be able to perceive a family resemblance linking them through traits they share with their parents.

Think of poetry in the same way. There is no obvious resemblance between

you left me
you left me
you left me
you left me
you left me
you left me
you left me
you left me
you left me
you left me
you left me
you left me
you left me
you left me
you left me
you left me
you left me

alone

and

> Slow, slow, fresh fount, keep time with my salt tears;
>   Yet slower yet, oh faintly, gentle springs;
> List to the heavy part the music bears,
>   Woe weeps out her division when she sings.
>   Droop herbs and flowers,
>   Fall grief in showers;
>   Our beauties are not ours;
>   Oh, I could still,
> Like melting snow upon some craggy hill,
>   Drop, drop, drop, drop,
> Since nature's pride is now a withered daffodil.*

---

* *Slow, slow, fresh fount* from the *Works of Benjamin Jonson, 1616,* in *Poetry of the English Renaissance,* Hebel and Hudson (Appleton-Century-Crofts, Inc., 1929), p. 514.

However these poems are linked through similarities with other poems such as this early (1663) shaped poem:

THE ALTAR *

A broken altar, Lord, thy servant rears,
Made of a heart and cemented with tears;
   Whose parts are as thy hand did frame;
   No workman's tool hath touched the same.
          A   heart   alone
          Is   such   a   stone
          As   nothing   but
          Thy power doth cut.
          Wherefore each part
          Of my hard heart
          Meets in this frame
          To prase thy name;
   That if I chance to hold my peace,
   These stones to praise thee may not cease.
Oh,   let   thy   blessed   sacrifice   be   mine,
And   sanctify   this   altar   to   be   thine.

and this experiment with spacing and punctuation:

most(people

simply

can't)
won't(most
parent people mustn't

shouldn't)most daren't

* *The Altar,* George Herbert from *The Temple,* 1633, in *Poetry of the English Renaissance,* Hebel and Hudson (Appleton-Century-Crofts, Inc., 1929), p. 727.

(sortof people well
youknow kindof)
aint

&

even
(not having
most ever lived

people always)don't

die(becoming most
buried unbecomingly
very

by

most)people *

Not only is there a wide, almost indefinable range of writings that are called poems, but also the line between poems and prose writing is not clear, nor need it be. When one looks at different forms in a flexible way it is no problem that a piece of writing may seem to have characteristics of poems and of nonpoems, or may mix elements of truth with elements of fiction, or may confound all classifications.

However there are some rough differences between different forms of writing that help the reader to orient him or herself when encountering an unfamiliar piece of writing that is placed in a certain tradition.

* #29 from e. e. cummings *Poems 1923–1954* (Harcourt Brace Jovanovich, 1972).

I will try my hand at making a list of family traits of those different forms of writing one is most likely to encounter:

poems

> —rhymes at the end of the lines or within lines
> —a weighing of each word or even syllable carefully according to sound as well as meaning
> —a free use of line breaks
> —the page looked at as a canvas to be used artistically rather than merely be filled up with print
> —an attention to images, to bringing together unfamiliar thoughts, ideas, objects, perceptions
> —use of comparisons (he is like a giraffe) and identification (he is a giraffe)
> —carefully controlled rhythm
> —condensation, cutting out of whole sentences
> —not bound to a particular moment in time

For each of these traits I can think of exceptions. I can also think of a novel that embodies almost all of them (Michel Butor's *Mobile U.S.A.*). However the traits are useful in pointing out aspects of poems that the reader can attend to in order to understand what the writer intends. These traits can be turned into questions the reader can ask him or herself while trying to become oriented to an unfamiliar form of writing. For example: Are there any rhymes or near rhymes? How are the words weighed— what does the poem sound like read aloud? How does the poem fit on the page? What picture does the poem make as a collection of black marks on a white page? What kind of images are used? Do they jar, please, puzzle?

fiction (novels, stories)
- —some disregard for history or fact
- —characters that never lived other than on the page
- —a story line, things happening, an elaboration of events
- —a storyteller or narrator
- —a setting, a freedom to create or change worlds, places, objects as well as people
- —an attempt to engage the reader, to teach or involve him or her in the story
- —a general dependence on complete sentences and paragraphs (sometimes this is deliberately avoided)
- —use of spoken language—either in the form of dialogue or in the form of an address to the reader

reporting or describing
- —use of whole sentences and paragraphs
- —keeping to actual events or people or to feelings about them
- —a pretense of there being no one talking (e.g. newspaper stories) or a clear identification of the writer as a real person (e.g. columnists)
- —a beginning, middle, and end
- —directness, the writer addressing the reader straightforwardly rather than using an imaginary voice (as in a lot of fiction)
- —using examples or instances

advertising
- —using language that reads quickly
- —using language to seduce/induce/trick the reader into acting in certain ways (i.e. buying things, going places, voting for people, etc.)

—boldness and cleverness
—use of contrasts or creating new meaning for famil-
    iar language
—trying to gain attention and be remembered
—variation of colors and sizes and shapes of letters
    to be unique

All of these lists can be turned into questions (as I did with some entries in the poem section) to help the reader take control of what is read and develop an ease with a variety of forms of writing. The questions can also give some insight into how writers work and make it easier for people to write themselves.

As an exercise to see what I mean here, pick an ad, read it, then ask yourself the following questions:

How quickly can you read it?
What does it try to make you do?
How bold or clever is it? (Be specific.)
What image or saying does it hinge on?
How does it grab your attention?
How are space, color, and shape used?

Then try to create a nonsense ad yourself using the same techniques used by the creator of the ad you just read. For example, write an ad to induce people to buy air, to induce them to dig holes, to convince them that dogs should have their own automobiles, to make them stop eating.

3. Voice

Consider the following first sentences of four very different books:

I got another barber that comes over from Carterville and helps me out Saturdays, but the rest of the time I can get along all right alone. You can see for yourself that this ain't no New York City and besides that, the most of the boys works all day and don't have no leisure to drop in here and get themselves prettied up.*

When my mother was pregnant with me, she told me later, a party of hooded Ku Klux Klan riders galloped up to our home in Omaha, Nebraska, one night. Surrounding the house, brandishing their shotguns and rifles, they shouted for my father to come out.†

Hip hole and hupmobile, Braunschweiger, you didn't invite Geiger and his counter for nothing, here is D.J. the friendLee voice at your service—hold tight young America—introductions come.**

I swear 'fo God this is the cussinges' man ever born, he must've been cussing when he came into this world, when his mother, Miss Lillybelle Washington, gave birth to this heathen the first thing he said must've been a cuss word, he probably cussed out the midwife and his mother and anybody else who happened to be in sight, cussed them out for bringin' him into the world, he is that kind of man, you know. . . .††

In each of these books the author establishes a distinct voice, whether his own or that of a particular character, right off. The voice that is speaking in the book gives the work character and style, and it is important for the reader to consider the voice that is telling a story as well

* Ring Lardner, *Haircut and Other Stories* (New York: Scribner's, 1949), p. 9.
† *The Autobiography of Malcolm X* (Grove Press, Inc., 1966), p. 1.
** Norman Mailer, *Why Are We In Vietnam?* (G. P. Putnam's, 1967), p. 7.
†† Cecil Brown, *The Life and Loves of Mr. Jiveass Nigger* (Farrar, Straus & Giroux, 1969), p. 1.

as the content of the story itself. There are many voices that are developed in writing, ranging from the highly personal voices of Norman Mailer or Malcolm X to the impersonal voice that is found in books that pretend to be "objective." The voice used in a written work reveals a great deal about what the author intends and about how the reader is to be treated. Some writers try to trick or seduce the reader into looking at the world through the author's eyes. Others try to keep the reader shifting perspective and therefore use many different voices to tell the story. Still others try to lead the reader to discover something about him or herself and therefore try to make their own voices as little intrusive as possible. As a reader begins to deal with more complex works there are some useful questions to raise with respect to voice:

> Who is speaking in the book?
> What are their biases and interests?
> How does the voice in the book relate to the voice of the author?
> What perspective is expected of the reader?
> What is the relationship of the voice telling the story to the reader? Are they intimate, hostile, indifferent?
> How does the voice play with language?

Sometimes it helps to read part of a book aloud and listen to the voice and guess at its rhythms and its sound. It is also useful to study one's own voice and try to transpose it into writing. Tell a story, then write it down in your own voice. Then work on the story so that it ends up reading smoothly as well as sounding like you. The best way to study voice in writing is to make an effort to develop your own voice. For many people writing is an unpleasant and unnatural activity. Though they may speak with ease, tell interesting stories and jokes, or be able to express their feelings with occasional eloquence, they panic when they face a blank sheet of paper. They cannot put their own voice into writing and so write in a labored, clumsy, and stiff manner.

Learning to write in school often makes the development of a personal writing voice difficult. The learner is presented with voiceless, bland models to imitate; he or she is told that some forms of writing such as business letters, job applications, term papers, etc., are expected to be bland, humorless, and styleless. Students are told to concentrate on grammar, spelling, punctuation, all of which in my mind are subordinate to voice. However there is no reason to become voiceless in *any* writing unless of course one chooses to parody a culture that deprives people of their voices.

A person who reads with ease can also begin to write with ease if he or she listens to him or herself, takes his or her voice seriously, and works on transposing it into writing. Of course people who learn to write and read together, and in a natural manner, don't have to struggle to find a voice in writing. The whole process of learning to read/write will also be for them the process of developing their own voices as well as being able to listen to others.

Exercises in the study of the written voice:

1. Study the first paragraph of a wide range of books.

2. Tell a simple tale (or take one from a book or news-

paper), then rewrite it with different voices. For example, describe a fire from the perspective of:

a dead victim

a witness

a fireman

an arsonist

a social scientist

Rewrite the story in the style of Mailer, Nabokov, anyone whose voice interests you.

3. Tape record a number of different people telling the same story or joke. Listen to the tape and pick out differences. Be specific—how do people's voices differ in vocabulary, experiences, sentence length, the images they choose, their own closeness or distance from what they are describing?

4. Make up dreams that you imagine different people may have and tell the dream in their words. For example, write out Richard Nixon's dream, Muhammed Ali's dream, a dog's dream, etc.

4. Test Taking

There are special skills involved in test taking and these are best learned after a person is already able to read with ease. You must make a clear distinction between being able to read well and being able to do well on tests (even reading tests). There are some people who can read intelligently and with ease and yet tighten up in the competitive atmosphere in which tests are usually given. There are others who have been trained to compete and do well though they hate reading and do not understand most of what they read.

There are compelling reasons to reject competitive and standardized tests altogether. However some tests at present give people access to jobs and scholarships and, therefore, one should probably know how to deal with them even while trying to eliminate them. The following skills can be taught fairly directly without confusing reading with test taking:

Figuring Out Instructions

Test instructions are usually couched in formal, uninteresting language and are hard to follow if one is nervous. It is best to get copies of old tests and go over instructions several times as well as rewrite them in more interesting language. There are certain things the copies give away about the tests. For example, when they say there is only one right answer to each question they are warning the reader not to be too clever. I know many kids who overlook obvious answers and come up with ingenious reasons for choosing answers that the test makers consider incorrect.

Instructions sometimes indicate whether it is best to guess or leave what you don't know blank. They also give simple questions and indicate how the sheet is to be marked. For many people the very form of the test and the answer sheets pose problems. The more familiar one is with the forms of questions and the look of test papers and answer sheets the easier they are to deal with.

One way to help learners is to get hold of sample tests and use the instructions as reading texts. Read them, vary them, ask students to make up sample questions.

Pretend you are a test giver and set up the social conditions under which tests are usually given. Help students get accustomed to the oppressive conditions under which they might have to function. And throw in some social analysis. If students understand that tests are used as weapons to exclude the disobedient and the nonconforming they will not have to look upon the test as a measure of the true worth of their soul or the quality of their intelligence.

Developing a Strategy

In high school I was taught how to take tests. The crucial thing was to learn how to deal with the test as a whole. I learned how to answer all the questions I was sure of first and how to mark those questions I was unsure of or didn't know at all. Many people are afraid to mark up the test sheet, which they treat as holy. However, you can do whatever is necessary to help yourself maximize your chances. I used to use a * for questions I wasn't sure of and a † for those that panicked me. Thus a question page might be coded like this:

1.
2.
*3.
*4.
5.
6.
†7.
8.
9.
†10.

This meant that I knew and answered 1,2,5,6,8, and 9. The answers to 3 and 4 could be worked on, and 7 and 10 were complete puzzles. If there was time I worked on 3 and 4 and left 7 and 10 for last. If guessing was to my advantage the unanswered questions could always be filled in by eliminating the most unlikely answers and choosing one of the remaining answers at random.

Imagining Who Made Up the Questions

It is important to understand that test makers were once test takers and they are often just getting even. Make up tests yourself—try to ask questions that people can answer, that they can't answer, that will humiliate or confuse them. Making a test is an act of certain people who value certain knowledge. If your values and those of the test makers do not coincide you will probably fail unless you care to play their game in order to secure the rewards they have to offer.

Practicing

Get a lot of test cram booklets—policemen's tests, bus drivers' tests, radio operators' tests, college entrance tests, high school equivalency tests—and practice. However, be sure not to confuse the particular skill of being able to do well on tests with other more substantial skills such as reading and writing.

Some Books on Level 3

Achebe, Chinua, *Things Fall Apart,* Fawcett, 1969.
Borges, Jorge Luis, with Margarita Guerrero, *The Book of Imaginery Beings,* Dutton, 1969.

Brooks, Gwendolyn, *In the Mecca,* Harper & Row, 1968.
Cobbs, Price, and William Grier, *Black Rage,* Basic Books, 1968.
Cruz, Victor Hernandez, *Snaps,* Vintage, 1970.
Deloria, Vine, Jr., *Custer Died for Your Sins: An Indian Manifesto,* Avon, 1970.
Grass, Günther, *The Tin Drum,* Signet, 1962.
Henderson, David, *The Mayor of Harlem,* Dutton, 1971.
The Autobiography of Malcolm X, Grove, 1964.
Marin, Peter, and Allan Y. Cohen, *Understanding Drug Use: An Adult's Guide to Drugs and the Young,* Harper & Row, 1971.
Strouse, Jean, *Up Against the Law—The Legal Rights of People under 21,* Signet, 1970.
Vassilikos, Vassilis, *Z,* Ballantine Books, 1969.

LEVEL 4: COMPLEX READING

LEVELS	SKILLS
Beginning	
Not Bad	
With Ease	
Complex	1. Knowing about languages 2. Special uses of words 3. Special languages 4. Critical analysis

No one ever reaches the stage where there is nothing left to learn about reading. There are always new forms of writing developing or shifts in old traditions that require adjustments on the part of the reader. There are technical vocabularies that may have to be mastered as well as the language of contracts, loans, and the civil and criminal law. Also the study of language itself is becoming increasingly sophisticated as are the techniques for the critical analysis of individual works.

1. Knowing About Languages

There is a difference between studying language and using the results of these studies to teach reading and writing. For example, it is one thing to study grammar and another to use grammar as a means of teaching writing. In my experience the obsession with grammar (diagraming sentences, breaking down sentences into parts which can be named) gets in the way of learning to write. It interferes with the development of a natural voice in writing and ease in reading. However the study of language is fascinating and people should be aware as much as possible of the nature and development of the medium they use the most.

It is probably easiest to pursue the serious study of language after one has already learned how to read, though one can also study language before or while learning how to read. It is just that the natural acquisition of the skills of reading and writing (which should develop hand in hand) don't require the formal use of grammar, structural linguistics, or any other practical teaching version of language theory.

The study of language has a number of aspects which can be pursued separately or integrated into a total study.

1. What is the structure of language systems? Are there any common structural features of all languages? How does the language work, how are sentences built up and changed? The study of these questions are variously called syntactics, structural linguistics, or linguistics. Books to look into:

Lyons, John, *Noam Chomsky,* The Viking Press, 1970.

More difficult and technical books on the subject:

Chomsky, Noam, *Cartesian Linguistics,* Harper & Row, 1966.
Chomsky, Noam, *Aspects of the Theory of Syntax,* MIT Press, 1965.
Harris, Zellig S., *Methods in Structural Linguistics,* University of Chicago Press, 1951.
Chomsky, Noam, and Halle, Morris. *The Sound Pattern of English,* Harper & Row, 1968.
Chomsky, Carol, *The Acquisition of Syntax in Children from 5 to 10,* MIT Press, 1969.

2. What are the meanings of words? How do meanings develop or change? How is it possible to understand the meaning of a sentence one has never heard before? The study of meanings is called semantics. Books to look into:

Lewis, C. S., *Studies in Words,* Cambridge University Press, 1967.
Oldfield, R. C., and Marshall, J. C., eds., *Language,* Penguin Books, Inc., 1968.

3. What kinds of signs are used to record spoken language? The study of signs is called semiotics. A few books:

Gelb, I. J., *A Study of Writing,* University of Chicago Press, 1952.
Cleator, P. E., *Lost Languages,* New American Library of World Literature, Inc., 1959.

4. How is language learned? What is there about the brain or soul that makes it possible for people to learn how to speak? What happens between infant and adult as the baby learns to talk? The study of the growth of the ability to speak is called developmental linguistics. Some books:

Vygotsky, L. S., *Thought and Language,* MIT Press, 1962.
Piaget, Jean, *The Language and Thought of the Child,* Meridian Books, 1955.
Smith, Frank, and Miller, George A., eds., *The Genesis of Language,* MIT Press, 1966.
Phillips, John L., Jr., *The Origins of Intellect: Piaget's Theory,* W. H. Freeman & Co., 1969.

More difficult and technical books on the subject:

Bellugi, Ursula, and Brown, Roger, eds., *The Acquisition of Language,* Serial No. 92, 1964 of the monographs of the Society for Research in Child Development, Purdue University, Lafayette, Indiana, 1964.
Chomsky, Carol, *The Acquisition of Syntax in Children from 5 to 10,* MIT Press, 1969.
Menyuk, Paula, *Sentences Children Use,* MIT Press, 1969.

5. How does language relate to thought? Does the language one speaks determine how one thinks or views the world? What is the psychology of speaking? The study of language and the mind is called psycholinguistics. Some books:

Oldfield, R. C., and Marshall, J. C., eds., *Language,* Penguin Books, Inc., 1968.
Smith, Frank and Miller, George A., eds., *The Genesis of Language,* MIT Press, 1966.

More difficult and technical books on the subject:

Lyons, J., and Wales, R. J., *Psycholinguistics Papers,* Proceedings
of the Edinburgh Conference, Edinburgh University Press, 1967.
Osgood, Charles E., and Sebeok, Thomas A., eds., *Psycholinguistics,* Indiana University Press, 1965.

6. How does language develop and change over long
periods of time? What happens to language when one
country conquers another? How do languages influence
each other when people speaking different tongues come
in contact through trade or war or love? This study is
called historical linguistics. Some books:

Oldfield, R.C., and Marshall, J. C., eds., *Language,* Penguin Books,
Inc., 1968.
Hogben, Lancelot, *The Mother Tongue,* Norton and Co., 1964.

7. How is language abused? How can it be used to trick
people or deceive them? How can language be used to
create belief in imaginary beings and objects? to perform
actions? to tell lies? How do specific terms like "right"
and "wrong" work in a language? The study of these
troublesome aspects of language is called philosophical
analysis or linguistic philosophy. Some books:

Flew, Antony, ed., *Logic and Language,* Doubleday and Co. Inc.,
1951.
Hare, R. M., *The Language of Morals,* Oxford University Press,
1952.
Wittgenstein, Ludwig, *Philosophical Investigations,* Macmillan,
1953.

8. What are the languages in the world like? Are they
all completely different or are there families of languages?

How do actual languages compare to each other? This study is called comparative linguistics.* Books to look at:

Alexandre, Pierre, *Languages and Language in Black Africa,* Northwestern University Press, 1972.

Hogben, Lancelot, *The Mother Tongue,* Norton and Co., 1964.

9. How does language relate to the structure of society? Socio-linguistics deals with this question. Some books:

Barnes, Douglas, *Language, the Learner and the School,* Penguin Papers in Education, 1969.

Vygotsky, L. S., *Thought and Language,* MIT Press, 1962.

A more difficult and technical book on the subject:

Capell, A., *Studies in Socio-Linguistics,* Mouton & Co., 1966.

Though everyone should be able to read and write on a complex level and know some basic information about one's language it is not necessary for everyone to be an expert on one of the above areas. In fact the subject is becoming so complex that I doubt if any one person can become an expert in all of them. The thing one has to worry about in our culture is the way in which most every new discovery or invention in the field of language study is pounced on by commercial manufacturers of reading and writing systems and turned into a teaching system. It is important to keep in mind the difference between analyzing language (or any other subject) and assuming that the results of the analysis solve the problem of learning.

---

* Naturally these categories overlap and so some books will appear on several lists.

2. Special Uses of Words

Sometimes neither a dictionary nor a thesaurus can help you figure out how a certain word is being used in a particular book. Some authors use special words in a personal and unique manner that can only be figured out as their meaning enfolds in the entire work. Such words as

racism	ego
dialectic	idea
moral	concept
thesis	consciousness
alienation	spirit
cooperation	

are used in different ways by different authors.

For example, Ludwig Wittgenstein in his *Philosophical Investigations* uses the words "use" and "meaning" in a very special way. At one point in the book he claims that the meaning of a word *is* its use. Then he proceeds to show what he means by developing a series of what he calls "language games." The dictionary meanings of "meaning," "use," "language," and "game" provide no insight into how Wittgenstein uses these words. In a sense one has to have read the whole book before reading it to fully understand what Wittgenstein is talking about. There are some books that are so beautiful they beg rereading. There are others that not merely beg rereading but demand it because of the complexity of ideas involved and the special way in which the author struggles to express his or her thoughts. The concepts of "alienation" and "dialectics" in Marx, the notion of "conscienization" in Freire, of "contradiction" in Mao, of "ideas" in Plato, of "God" in many works, all fall into this class.

There is a special skill involved in reading through a
book trying to understand how certain concepts are used,
and then rereading it to get a sense of the whole work. At
this stage reading is good hard work. Sometimes this kind
of reading is best done with a few friends who are trying
to understand the nuances of a work that has common
interest. A group of us, for example, will be trying to
puzzle out Paolo Freire's *The Pedagogy of the Oppressed*
this fall. We will all read the same chapter, raise questions, entertain various interpretations, push each other.
There is no question of a teacher-student relationship
being involved, unless of course we look upon the book as
the teacher. The group got together because of a common
need and not because of any institutional ties.

People often fail to realize that they can come together
to learn something new even if they don't belong to a school
or have a professional teacher around. In our culture we
undervalue our own and each other's knowledge and intelligence and fall into the habit of being led. The way to
break this habit is by breaking it. If you want to learn
something and know someone who knows it ask him or her
to teach you. If no one knows what you want to learn or
understand, get some friends together and puzzle it out
together.

3. Special Languages

The law has its own vocabulary and requires a special
way of being read. The same is true for medicine, the
sciences, technology, and a lot of contemporary poetry
and fiction. When dealing with an unfamiliar form of writing it makes sense to spend some time figuring out the

system used. There are some questions one can ask oneself:

1. Which words in this area are being used in a special way (i.e. differently than they are used in ordinary language)?

2. Are there any new words that have been created in this form? Why?

3. What area of life or thought is the work dealing with?

4. What are its assumptions about people? Objects?

5. Does the language used seem deliberately over-technical, as if it were intended to hide something from people who haven't been initiated into the profession?

6. Can the content you read be reduced to simpler language? Try to do it.

Most people will not have to read many technical or scientific works in their lives. However they will have to relate in some way to leases, contracts, loan papers, and other legal documents. If you don't understand what you sign you're an easy mark for exploitation. It is important for people to command the law rather than be subjects of it and in this instance reading is not merely desirable but necessary. I think part of the equipment of anyone who teaches reading (especially to people older than ten) should be a brief case filled with legal forms to be used as reading texts.

4. Critical Analysis

There are a number of different ways of looking at any written material. For example, one can consider a work in terms of:

1. The work itself, the language it uses, the ideas it seems to express;
2. The social and political context in which it was written and the audience it was intended for (for example, whether it was meant to entertain the rich, amuse the academic, educate the masses, etc.);
3. The tradition of writing it comes out of (for example, how a contemporary poem relates to other contemporary poetry or to previous poetry; and
4. The view of the world presented or implied in the work, or the author's philosophy or way of perceiving reality.

Each of these ways of considering writing has given rise to a tradition of literary analysis, and each way has its partisans. For my part, if a work is sufficiently important to a person it should be examined from as many different aspects as possible. People who are serious about reading ought to become familiar with some of the different traditions of analyzing novels and poems and other forms of writing. Some useful books on criticism are:

Cardwell, Christopher, *Studies and Further Studies in a Dying Culture,* Monthly Review Press, 1971.
Caute, David, *The Illusion,* Harper & Row, 1972.
Ellman, Richard, *Eminent Domain,* Oxford University Press, Galaxy Books, 1970.
Forster, E. M., *Aspects of Criticism,* Vintage.
Hollander, John, ed., *Modern Poetry: Essays in Criticism,* Oxford University Press, Galaxy Books, 1968.
Lowenthal, Leo, *Literature and the Image of Man,* Beacon Press, 1966.

Lukacs, George, *Realism in Our Time,* Harper Torchbooks, 1971.
Olson, Charles, *Selected Writing,* ed. Robert Greeley, New Directions.
Sontag, Susan, *Against Interpretation,* Dell, 1969.

Some books on the complex level:

Casteneda, Carlos, *The Teachings of Don Juan,* University of California, Berkeley, 1969.
Churchman, C. West, *The Systems Approach,* Delta, 1968.
Freire, Paolo, *Pedagogy of the Oppressed,* Herder & Herder, 1971.
Goffman, Erving, *The Presentation of Self in Everyday Life,* Doubleday Anchor, 1959.
Malinowski, Bronislaw, *The Family Among the Australian Aborigines,* Schocken, 1963.
Marcuse, Herbert, *One Dimensional Man,* Beacon, 1964.
Marx, Karl, *Capital,* Modern Library.
Reed, Ishmael, *The Free-Lance Pallbearers,* Bantam, 1969.
Rukeyser, Muriel, *The Traces of Thomas Hariot,* Random House, 1971.
Steiner, George, *In Bluebeard's Castle,* Yale University Press, 1971.

At this point a look at the whole breakdown of the process of learning to read makes sense. It is important to remember that this is not the only way to look at reading. Nor does it exhaust every aspect of reading. It is what I know of reading. I believe there is enough here and in the subsequent sections of this book to enable people with no previous teaching experience to help others learn how to read. I also expect it may be of use to some professional teachers.

So far I have concentrated almost exclusively on mastery of the language skills that go into the ability to read. However, there are other things about learning how to read that should be considered *on each of the four levels* by people trying to help others learn to read.

Levels	Skills
Beginning	1. Knowing print 2. Known words 3. Words that connect and words that place 4. Alphabet 5. Sounds and combinations of sounds 6. Simple sentences
Not Bad	1. Combinations of sounds 2. Complicated words 3. Complex sentences 4. Everyday reading 5. Paragraphs and stories
With Ease	1. Unfamiliar words 2. Different forms of writing 3. Voice 4. Test taking
Complex	1. Knowing about language 2. Special uses of words 3. Special languages 4. Critical analysis

It is important to consider (1) the learner's confidence in him or herself, (2) the understanding the learner has of the process of reading, of life, and of the written word, and (3) the learner's physical conditioning—specifically the speed with which he or she reads and his or her ability to read with concentration for a period of time. Adding these conditions to the chart I have drawn of the process of learning to read (*see page 134*).

These psychological, intellectual, and physical dimensions of learning to read need some elaboration.

Skills	Confidence	Understanding			Physical Conditioning	
		Strategy	Street Understanding	Book Understanding	Speed	Stamina
Beginning 1. 2. 3. 4. 5. 6.						
Not Bad 1. 2. 3. 4. 5.						
With Ease 1. 2. 3. 4.						
Complex 1. 2. 3. 4.						

The Confidence of the Learner

It is necessary to try to understand how the learner feels about his or her capacity to learn how to read. Is the learner overconfident or totally lacking in confidence? Does he or she feel stupid and get nervous in the presence of the printed word? For example, I have noticed certain nervous habits that often indicate someone who feels defeated about learning to read:

1. eyes constantly shifting away from the text making it impossible to get absorbed in the text
2. constant drumming or shaking of the feet while trying to read
3. nervous tremors, a stammering or pleading voice
4. sweaty hands and perspiration on the forehead
5. constant farting or coughing or clearing the throat

Being convinced you can't learn how to read is no joke. Many young people leave school feeling defeated and stupid. They fear books and are convinced that reading is beyond their capacity.

These victims of our schools are usually intact in other areas of their lives. It is as if they had a reading phobia the way other people have snake phobias or height problems.

The person who wants to teach must be sensitive to the learner's feelings of inferiority without at the same time indulging or confirming them. The learner's intelligence can easily be insulted if he or she is treated as sick or retarded or helpless. The strategy that works best in my experience is telling people directly what you see. Let them know how the schools have screwed them; how they have become convinced of their own failure; and how that attitude gets in the way of learning. Point out nervous habits you discover, without being cruel, but with the conviction that they can learn. If you don't believe someone can learn from you don't try to teach them. You'll only screw them up more. It is inhuman to experiment on people or to create circumstances where their failure is manufactured.

There is one other thing to look at: does the learner read with confidence on a simple level and yet lose confidence when new and more difficult material is encountered? Here the problem is helping the learner how to learn and to deal with new experience. Once again, the most useful strategy for the teaching person is to tell the learner what the problem seems to be. In my experience the more people understand about the process of reading and about themselves as learners with socially induced problems, the easier it is for them to work their way out of these problems.

Understanding

Strategy:

Knowing what to do with material you've never seen before. There are at least four ways of encountering something that one does not know. One way is to *panic*, a second is to *evade*, a third is to *cope*, and a fourth is to *deal*.

Panicking. A reader who panics facing new material flees the written page—the reader throws the book on the floor or accuses it of being stupid. He or she may turn on the teacher or run out of the room or roll into a ball or cry with frustration.

For some people the admission that they don't know something causes so much anxiety that they must destroy the situation. When a person is that devastated by failure with reading, anyone who would help them has to provide ways for the learner to begin all over again with reading. If the person fears books try comics, if they fear comics try signs or advertisements. If he or she panics at the sight of any written material try chess or checkers and move slowly into writing about those games. Find the person's strengths and interests and build from there. Try to neutralize or randomize the learner's past experience with reading so that the habit of panicking can be overcome. And of course tell him or her what you are doing and why you are doing it.

Evading. Some people have developed the most ingenious techniques for avoiding reading. For example, they pretend to have read everything, or listen carefully to what other people say about books and bluff their way through school. When faced with new material in the presence of a teacher they can talk your ear off and charm your pants off without even getting near the book.

Evasion is in some ways more difficult to deal with than panic. People who evade reading tend to be extremely good with words and can sit and discuss reading or their problems for hours, all the talk being part of the process of avoiding dealing with some material that is unfamiliar.

Many people who evade reading at the same time want to learn how to read but are too proud to accept help or admit they don't know something. My strategy has been to talk about reading with such people, guess at what they are avoiding, give them hints in an offhand manner, and then leave them alone to figure out how to put it together.

For example, I have known people too proud to admit that they don't know how to look up a word in a dictionary. In talking with them I usually pick up a dictionary, look up some word myself describing aloud what I'm doing (e.g. for the word "justice" getting the j's and then going to the ju's and then to the jus's), and then leave the dictionary around. Some people need indirect teaching or teaching by example. Provide them with an example of how to do something and leave them alone. They'll figure it out for themselves.

Coping. Coping consists of skipping over unfamiliar material or guessing at it and moving on. Coping may also be learning to recognize some words in print while never bothering to find out their pronunciation. For example, while reading a foreign novel many strange seemingly unpronounceable names may be encountered. A reader could cope with the names by remembering the first three letters of each name. However, coping could get you confused if many characters in the book have names beginning with the same three letters.

Coping sometimes makes sense. There are times when a story is so absorbing that stopping to puzzle out the meaning of each unfamiliar word can ruin one's whole experience with the work. It is only when coping rather than actually dealing with the unfamiliar becomes a habit that trouble with reading can develop. If one only guesses at unfamiliar words and never asks someone else, or never uses the dictionary, one is likely to guess wrong at times and become confused and frustrated. People who are able to read well enough to cope, however, can easily learn how to deal.

Dealing. Knowing how to deal with unfamiliar material consists of different things on the different levels of reading. At the beginning level, for example, it consists of knowing how to sound out some simple words never before encountered. It consists of knowing how words are put together from sounds and how sentences are built from words. On the other levels it consists of knowing more about the process of reading, of being able to use resources such as the dictionary and thesaurus, and finally of being able to admit that there are things one doesn't know and ask for help.

A person needn't deal with every unfamiliar word or reference in a book. The important thing is knowing how to deal when one wants to.

Street Understanding:

There are very few people incapable of learning to read. Perhaps some brain-injured and severely retarded individuals qualify. But anyone who can navigate on the streets, who knows how to survive, who can talk, who has interests in building, cooking, hustling, bullshitting, joking, playing, exploring, can learn to read. The teacher must know something of the everyday lives of the learners in order to build a program based on the familiar and natural associations people have with print as well as with their personal interests.

In our culture people use easily words like "stupid," "damaged," "disadvantaged," "slow," "retarded," "educationally handicapped." No one who cares to help others learn can afford to use the words except in the most extreme cases. If you cannot help someone learn leave it at that. Do not project your own failure onto the learner.

To avoid slipping into accusing learners find out about

their lives. How are their hours and minutes occupied? How do they use their minds during the course of the day? What do they have to figure out in order to survive? What understanding of people do they command? What kind of stories do they tell or like to hear? And how do you do these same things? Be specific and detailed about people's lives and it will be difficult to use abstract categories and labels to put them down.

Book Understanding:

How well do people understand what they read? Do they think about what they read, talk to other people, compare different works? Do they think independently and critically about what they read? Book understanding is not really a separate dimension of learning to read. Reading consists among other things of understanding. However when the material people are expected to read is dull, pretentious, silly, there isn't much for them to think about. The more basal the reading material, the more reading becomes an automatic skill rather than an act of understanding.

At all the levels of reading it is important to take time to talk and think about what is being read, to integrate the material into one's life.

Comprehension is not, as the schools seem to make it, the ability to pick the best title of a paragraph or the correct meaning of a sentence. Rather it is the ability to put together an intelligent and plausible inerpretation of what the author is saying, and then to consider other interpretations critically. It is the ability to search for meaning and think about what one has read. A teacher who does not think about books him or herself can not help others do it.

Physical Conditioning for Reading

Speed:

I am not a speed reading freak. I like to read leisurely, put down the book and think, let my mind wander. Some material that interests me has to be read very slowly since it is highly specialized and requires a lot of thought. Other material such as the sports page of the *San Francisco Chronicle* I can rip right through. The speed with which I read depends upon the material being read and to some extent the way I feel while reading. However I read well enough for my purposes and don't feel a need for speed reading.

People must set their own comfortable pace for reading and vary that pace according to their ability to understand what they are reading. Speed reading might be desirable for some but doesn't seem necessary to me.

However, beginning readers have to develop a pace and often get stuck by reading each word as if it had no relationship to other words and lose the meaning of sentences and paragraphs. Try to read the following sentence aloud a word at a time, pronouncing each word with the same tone:

> If / he / went / to / the / store / he / might /
> meet / that / strange / old / man / he / has
> / been / talking / about /.

Now read it with the following breaks:

> If he went / to the store / he might / meet /
> that strange old man / he has been / talking about.

Reading groups of words that fall together in speech as units helps develop speed. However as experience with reading grows whole sentences can be read much the way they would be spoken. At this point the learner can stop worrying about the mechanics of reading and attend more carefully to meaning.

Think of how you listen to someone who is talking to you. Somehow all at the same time you take in the tone of the voice, the speed with which he or she is talking, the rhythm of his or her language, the gesture he or she is making, the words themselves, and the meaning of what is being said. The entire process happens too quickly and immediately for you to hear words or even phrases separately. The whole of the act of speech is understood at one time. To prove this to yourself try to concentrate on each individual word in a conversation. Then try to concentrate on groups of words. Then on rhythm, etc. As you pay attention to one component most likely you will lose sight of the meaning of the whole.

Try this experiment with people who are learning how to read. Then let them do the same thing with reading: try a word at a time; then try groups of words; then try to read attending not to the process of reading but to the sound and meaning of the words.

The development of comfortable speed (as opposed to word-by-word reading or reading disconnected groups of words) is not difficult but requires practice. That is why I list speed as an aspect of physical conditioning for reading. One learns to read with reasonable speed by reading.

Stamina:

Most people get tired after reading for several hours. Their heads spin, concentration disappears, they feel tired and almost physically exhausted. It is amazing how much physical energy can be expended while sitting still, look-ing, and thinking. This statement may seem absurd until you think that a chess champion like Bobby Fischer can lose between five and ten pounds in a two-hour chess game and has to train as hard physically for a chess match as a boxer does for a prize fight.

Not only do we all have limits to how long we can read, but also these limits shift with the difficulty of the material being read. However, there are some people who have no stamina to speak of for reading. For example, they may be able to read one page with good speed and ease and under-standing and then fall apart on the second page. Some kids I know who have bad experiences with reading in school even forget letters, reverse words (i.e. read "no" as "on," "now" as "won," "saw" as "was," etc.), stumble, get nervous, and fall apart altogether after just a few para-graphs.

For the most part these young people have been so turned off that they don't read and therefore never build up any stamina. However, it is possible to suggest that people push themselves a bit farther every day. There is no rush—in my experience small changes over long periods of time are more effective than attempts to change over-night. For example, find out how much of a certain book a person can read comfortably. Then suggest they read an extra sentence the first night, an extra two the next night. Another way to build stamina is to have people reread favorite books in larger and larger sections at one sitting. I have even resorted to suggesting that people read the names in the telephone book, or menus, or any other fairly simple material to develop staying power as readers. Stamina is something the reader has to develop for him or herself, but it need not be a problem once it is pointed out as something to be worked on.

Let's take another look at the chart I've laid out as a guide to understanding reading. The chart is merely a convenient way of setting out what I know about reading. Because something appears earlier or later does not mean that learning takes place in that order. If some aspects of reading have been left out fill them in. If something noted on the chart is of no use disregard it. If the very notion of a chart repels you take whatever is of value to you from the discussion and forget the chart. If on the other hand you feel a need to place yourself and your students in some framework use it as you see fit. However, understand that this IS NOT A SYSTEM, it is merely a personal sketch based on one person's experiences teaching reading. Don't fall into the trap of making it into a system and then believing its use will automatically turn out readers. You'll be disappointed, most likely feel cheated, and end up looking for another formula, which will also fail. For the most part people teach themselves how to read with a little help from their friends, especially if their friends know a little bit more than they do about reading. Learn what you can about reading, use whatever you can get your hands on, and try to be of some use to someone else. Listen carefully to the person you would help, discover what they already know, and begin there.

A note for people who have to prove to others that they are doing something about reading, or an alternative to standardized tests:

Many people involved in developing new ways of teaching and learning are under pressure to give proof that they are doing responsible work and that their students are learning. This is especially true for schools or literacy programs that have to be responsive to poor communities and for alternative institutions that receive public money. The usual way of measuring students' learning in reading is to give standardized tests of reading twice a year and then measure "growth" by the difference in the scores. For example, a student might get a 5.6 in September and a 6.5 in June, supposedly indicating nine months reading growth during the school year. There are, however, a number of serious problems that make standardized tests worthless:

1. They are racist. The language and world they represent is middle class, stiff, formal, unpleasant, overly verbal.

2. They measure nondefined levels of reading growth. There is no such thing as a 6.5 as opposed to 6.4 or 6.6 level of reading. These numbers were developed by averaging out the results of applying the test to a sample of students (the so-called normalizing or standardizing group) so that scores would come out in years and months to fit the number of years and months in the school year. The numbers do not have meaning in terms of the process of reading.

3. The ability to do well on tests is a special skill, which may or may not relate to the ability to read. The setting in which the test is given, the person who gives it, the nervous state of the test taker, the way the instructions are read, familiarity with the type of questions asked, the weather— all contribute to determining the test results. A person

can score a 6.5 on one day and a 5.9 or 6.9 on another. What does that tell about his or her reading? *

4. The test results do not help the student or teacher to know exactly how the student reads. Consider the following simple question from a standardized test:

Circle the one that matches.

ball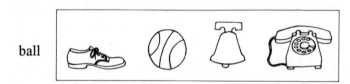

Suppose the student circles the ball and gets the answer right. There are two possible reasons: (1) he or she understood the directions, read the word correctly, saw the right picture or (2) he or she guessed.

Suppose the student got the wrong answer. There are even more possibilities: (1) he or she didn't understand the instructions and panicked; (2) he or she read "ball" as "bell" and circled the bell; (3) he or she read "ball" as "call" and circled the telephone; or (4) he or she guessed incorrectly.

The result of the test says nothing about how the student arrived at that score.

5. Finally, the test is a competitive instrument. It indicates how well someone competes with respect to other students. It shifts the focus away from the process of reading onto the process of competing.

* It should be noted, however, that in a gross way the test can give some hints about reading. For example, if the students in a "rich" school have no problem dealing with the test while the kids in a "poor" school in the same city all hit the bottom of the scale something is wrong and must be dealt with. However, that gross fact does not justify using the test.

There is no need to go into criticism of standardized tests with any greater detail. The problem is how to replace them by a more sensible way of indicating whether a person is learning or not. I have been reluctant to try my hand at developing an alternative to testing. Basically trust should exist between student and teacher, or student, teacher, and parent and the word should be the vehicle of evaluation. If a teacher is capable of admitting failure, if he or she is not interested in mystifying or deceiving students and community, there should be no need for elaborate documents. However no such trust exists. Poor communities have been so cheated by the schools that they would be insane to trust educators. And, of course, there is a need to justify the use of public money in an "objective" way in our culture. So I've tried my hand at developing ways of describing how well a person reads either in his or her own or someone else's judgment, and also of showing whether he or she develops as a reader. The processes I will describe use the chart evolved in this section of the book, and are not bound to a school situation. They can be used on the streets, at home, for oneself or one's friends. It is important to get away from the notion that finding out how well someone does in reading should be confined to the formal setting of the school.

Consider my schema for describing the components of learning to read keeping the following things in mind:

1. In the skills columns the order is not developmental. It is not as if one must know informal words (Beginning —2) before the alphabet (Beginning—3), or know different forms of writing (With Ease—2) before considering test taking (With Ease—4). Many things are learned at the same time and in different ways by different people.

Those components could just as well not have been numbered.

2. The methods of helping someone learn the skills on the chart may be quite different from the ones I suggested, while the chart itself might still be of use.

3. The chart may be incomplete, redundant, not appropriate—feel free to make your own or devise another method altogether.

4. The chart does not represent a system, it is just a convenient way of summarizing and relating a lot of information about reading that should be made available to parents, teachers, students, authorities, etc.

It is possible to develop the chart in a number of ways so that one can see at a glance how well a person reads. Let me go one column at a time (*see facing page*).

Levels

The first thing one may want to do is determine the level on which a person reads. These levels are not completely distinct, their boundaries tend to fade into each other. Someone who has mastered most of the skills of beginning reading most likely has started to read on the not bad level. However the levels can be separated well enough to make a reasonably accurate judgment about where to place a reader (one, by the way, that a number of people would agree upon). If someone seems to be on the line between two levels that can be indicated too.

I have indicated what I mean by these different levels in the text and have given lists of books and other printed material that go with them. However any group of people trying to use this chart ought to find its own material.

	Skills	Confidence	Strategy	Understanding		Physical Conditioning	
				Street Understanding	Book Understanding	Speed	Stamina
Beginning	1. Knowing print 2. Known words 3. Words that connect and words that place 4. Alphabet 5. Sounds and combinations of sounds 6. Simple sentences	none not much enough	Panics Evades Copes Deals	Not at all With problems OK	Not at all With problems OK	Very slow Slow OK Speed freak	No stamina Problems w/ stamina OK Stamina freak
Not Bad	1. Combinations of sounds 2. Complicated words 3. Complex sentences 4. Everyday reading 5. Paragraphs and stories	none not much enough	Panics Evades Copes Deals	Not at all With problems OK	Not at all With problems OK	Very slow Slow OK Speed freak	No stamina Problems w/ stamina OK Stamina freak
With Ease	1. Unfamiliar words 2. Different forms of writing 3. Voice 4. Test taking	none not much enough	Panics Evades Copes Deals	Not at all With problems OK	Not at all With problems OK	Very slow Slow OK Speed freak	No stamina Problems w/ stamina OK Stamina freak
Complex	1. Knowing about language 2. Special uses of words 3. Special languages 4. Critical analysis	none not much enough	Panics Evades Copes Deals	Not at all With problems OK	Not at all With problems OK	Very slow Slow OK Speed freak	No stamina Problems w/ stamina OK Stamina freak

Several schools in Berkeley have used the chart as a means of reporting on reading and have defined these levels through printed material that seemed relevant to their students. The teachers at the schools brought in ten books each ranging from simple to highly complex, went through the books and sorted them into four piles according to some of the descriptions given in the chart. The books were chosen according to the interests of the students and the philosophy of each of the schools. For example, Casa de la Raza used some books in Spanish as well as works by Chicanos. Black House put an emphasis on contemporary black literature.

After looking at the books the staff set up a diagnostic table in each school with the four piles of books on each table. Each student was shown the chart, and the breakdown of reading was discussed. It was assumed, an uncommon thing in most schools, that the students were intelligent enough to know as much as they cared to about the process of reading. Many young people who resisted formal testing of any sort became interested in the process of finding out where they were since there was nothing hidden or threatening about the situation and since the result was not some number indicating inferiority or superiority.

The students were asked to choose a book to read, to practice if they wanted to, to start easy or hard—however they chose—and to read to a staff member of their choice. Over a period of a few weeks all of the students in each of the four schools had read several times (mostly aloud, in a few cases silently followed by discussing the book) and a level had been found.

It is interesting that some high school students who read

on a beginning level commented that being a beginning reader felt different than being a 2.6 reader since 2.6 implied they had the intelligence of second-graders while beginning implied nothing about their intelligence.

Sometimes it is not necessary to go through even the informal procedure described above to find out how well someone reads. Most teachers who listen to their students know at what level their students are.

Skills

Through reading with someone or through playing language games or by asking it is possible to find out what reading skills a person has or lacks. The more one observes the more one learns. My skills breakdown can be used as a checklist to help place a reader if it makes sense for your purposes to be more specific than placing him or her simply on a level. For each skill it probably makes sense to give one of three indications:

√ —knows it

X —has no. idea

O —has some mastery and is working on it

Thus part of two profiles of beginning readers might look like the chart on page 152.

In some cases one may even want to get more specific and attach a sheet indicating what seems to be known or not known. For example, in the case of a reader who is having trouble with the alphabet a checklist with the letters marked off that are causing trouble may be of use, both to have a record for the teacher and more important as a help for the student. As I mentioned before in the book

1			2		
Levels	Skills		Levels	Skills	
(Beginning)	1. ✓ 2. ✓ 3. ✓ 4. ✓ 5. ✓ 6. O		(Beginning)	1. ✓ 2. ✓ 3. X 4. X 5. O 6. O	
Not Bad	1. 2. 3. 4. 5.		Not Bad	1. 2. 3. 4. 5.	
With Ease	1. 2. 3. 4.		With Ease	1. 2. 3. 4.	
Complex	1. 2. 3. 4.		Complex	1. 2. 3. 4.	

there need be no separation between discovering what a student doesn't know and telling or helping him or her discover it. Diagnosis and learning should not be separate activities.

I think it is important not to be overspecific. Any information collected should be of use to the student. The more miscellaneous information collected the more there is a tendency to put the information in order. From that order there is a small but dangerous step to believing that your order is *the* order in which things *must* be learned.

It is possible to begin with an open, sensitive, student-oriented perspective and end up caught into a schema you have a lot of stake in and therefore elevate into being the TRUTH about learning.

Confidence

On each level a learner may or may not have confidence, or may fit anywhere in between. It is possible to develop a continuum from 0 to 1—0 meaning no confidence and 1 meaning confidence that one can learn. Then confidence can be judged to be on the line.

$$
\begin{array}{ll}
0 \quad \bullet & \leftarrow \\
\quad | & \text{or} \\
1 \quad \bullet & \leftarrow
\end{array}
$$

One can also determine 7 or 5 or 6 or 3 or any degree of confidence. For my purposes it has been adequate to use three simple descriptions: none, not much, and enough. Thus a sample profile including the aspect of confidence might look like the chart on page 154.

Understanding

Strategy.

In accordance with my previous discussion this section has been divided into:

panics —P
evades—E
copes —C
deals —D

Levels	Skills	Confidence
(Beginning)	1. √ 2. √ 3. X 4. O 5. X 6. X	None Not much * Enough
Not Bad	1. 2. 3. 4. 5.	None Not much Enough
With Ease	1. 2. 3. 4.	None Not much Enough
Complex	1. 2. 3. 4.	None Not much Enough

Street understanding and book understanding have been divided much the way confidence was divided:

    not at all   —N
    with problems—P
    OK   —OK

My tendency is to keep things as simple as possible and depend upon judgment. I think the worst thing that could happen would be to try to assume that there are only three levels of understanding books and then define them so that a machine could determine which level a person is on. In teaching as in much of life judgment must be exercised with the awareness that one might always be wrong. It is no tragedy if you misplace a student—if you made a mistake correct it and apologize.

A sample profile including the dimension of understanding:

	Skills	Confidence	Strategy	Understanding — Street Understanding	Understanding — Book Understanding
(Beginning)	1. ✓ 2. ✓ 3. X 4. O 5. X 6. X	None / Not much * / Enough	Panics / Evades * / Copes / Deals	N / P / OK *	N * / P / OK
Not Bad	1. 2. 3. 4. 5.	n / nm / e	P / E / C / D	N / P / OK	N / P / OK
With Ease	1. 2. 3. 4.	n / nm / e	P / E / C / D	N / P / OK	N / P / OK
Complex	1. 2. 3. 4.	n / nm / e	P / E / C / D	N / P / OK	N / P / OK

Physical Conditioning

Speed:

In accordance with my previous discussion of speed in reading this aspect has been broken down into four parts:

> reads a word at a time—very slow—VS
> reads a few words at a time—slow—S
> reads comfortably—OK
> a speed freak——SF

Stamina:

No stamina (NS) means someone who falls apart after a few sentences or paragraphs. Problems with stamina (PS) means someone who can only read a few pages at a time. (OK) means someone who can read a short story or several chapters of a book at a sitting. A stamina freak (SF) is someone who can read a book at one sitting.

Now lets look at a completed profile (*see facing page*).

Just looking at the profile it is clear that the person is practically a nonreader. However, there is some confidence, a command of an informal vocabulary, an awareness of how print is oriented on the page, and a good head for survival. There is also an indication that the person is clever enough to evade the issue of reading whenever possible. From the profile and some additional information (how old the person is, what he or she is interested in, where he or she lives? perhaps) one can begin to suggest a program. Of course, if you know the person the profile might not be necessary.

Suppose the person were twelve, interested in pigeons and racing cars; it would then be possible to put together

	Skills	Confidence	Understanding			Physical Condition	
			Strategy	Street Understanding	Book Understanding	Speed	Stamina
(Beginning)	1. ✓ 2. ✓ 3. ✗ 4. ○ 5. ✗ 6. ✗	n nm e	P E C D	N P OK	N P OK	VS S OK SF	NS PS OK SF
Not Bad	1. 2. 3. 4. 5.	n nm e	P E C D	N P OK	N P OK	VS S OK SF	NS PS OK SF
With Ease	1. 2. 3. 4.	n nm e	P E C D	N P OK	N P OK	VS S OK SF	NS PS OK SF
Complex	1. 2. 3. 4.	n nm e	P E C D	N P OK	N P OK	VS S OK SF	NS PS OK SF

a program using the informal vocabulary, words and
images taken from the worlds of pigeons and cars as well
as car repair manuals and pigeon training books, the list
of place words, etc. It would also make sense to talk about
the strategies used to avoid reading, and to take advantage
of the student's street knowledge by having him or her
dictate or tape record and transcribe stories and tales that
would be beyond his or her reading capacity and then use
them as reading texts. In a few months significant changes
might take place with as little as one hour a week's work
with a teaching person if the learner is serious. Many
people are hung-up on measuring or at least specifying
change and the charts might be used over a period of time
to indicate how someone is doing. Here, for example, may
be what the profile under consideration would look like
after six months (*see facing page*).

This indicates that the person has learned the alphabet
as well as the connecting words and can begin to deal
with sentences. His or her confidence has increased, reading is no longer evaded and some understanding of the
written word as well as speed and stamina has developed.
Change has been indicated this way without necessarily
having to be indicated by numbers that cannot be translated into human terms.

ONE SUGGESTION: Before using this or any other version
of the chart try to translate a number of imaginary profiles into ordinary language. Write down what you think
they say. Ask some friend to do the same thing and compare versions. Make sure you don't invest the chart with
a meaning itself and somehow look to it to solve your
problems. *Always consider the age and experience of the*

	Skills	Confidence	Strategy	Understanding		Physical Condition	
				Street Understanding	Book Understanding	Speed	Stamina
Beginning	1. ✓ 2. ✓ 3. ✗ 4. O 5. ✗ 6. ✗	n nm e	P E C D	N P OK	N P OK	VS S OK SF	VS S OK SF
Not Bad	1. 2. 3. 4. 5.	n nm e	P E C D				
With Ease	1. 2. 3. 4.						
Complex	1. 2. 3. 4.						

——————— initial profile

----------- six months later

person you are talking about. The chart may have to be used—IT IS NOT NECESSARY.

Here are a few imaginary profiles along with some additional information about the supposed learners. Try to write out what they tell you and also what you might do. Think of several ways to proceed in each case. Some questions you might ask yourself:

1. What are the person's strengths?
2. What can be suggested so the learner can depend upon me as little as possible?
3. What activities involving print can be done by the learner

    at home
    on the streets
    in school
  alone
  with two or three friends
  with lots of friends
  with a teaching person

        one on one
        in small groups
        with a whole class

  with parents

      by wandering around and looking
      copying words
      asking questions

4. What printed resources exist in the learner's community? How can they be used?
5. Do you feel you can be of use to this particular person or should you find someone else to help him or her?

Imaginary Profile 1: This is the profile of a sixteen-year-old Chicano woman who is interested in going to college and becoming a teacher. She speaks Spanish and English, lives in a predominantly Chicano lower-middle-class neighborhood in Los Angeles. (*See page 162*)

your analysis:

several programs: 1.   2.

Imaginary Profile 2: This is the profile of a twelve-year-old black girl who is interested in becoming a scientist. She lives in a racially mixed middle-class neighborhood in the Bronx. (*See page 163*)

your analysis:

several programs:

Group Profiles

Sometimes it might be necessary to provide a group portrait of reading skills. In the Berkeley public alternative schools there has been considerable pressure to get school-by-school and class-by-class pictures of reading development. The most logical way to do this would be to look at all the individual profiles to see whether some students began with reading trouble and have not moved. However bureaucrats don't have time to look at the development of each student and therefore want group measures. This provides problems. The more general one gets the less one sees individuals and the more useless the information becomes. There are ways to satisfy the bureau-

	Skills	Confidence	Understanding			Physical Condition	
			Strategy	Street Understanding	Book Understanding	Speed	Stamina
Beginning	1. 2. 3. 4. 5. 6.						
Not Bad	1. O 2. O 3. O 4. O 5. O	n nm e	P E C D	N P OK	N P OK	VS S OK SF	NS S OK SF
With Ease	1. 2. 3. 4.						
Complex	1. 2. 3. 4.						

| | Skills | Understanding | | | | Physical Condition | |
		Confidence	Strategy	Street Understanding	Book Understanding	Speed	Stamina
Beginning	1. 2. 3. 4. 5. 6.						
Not Bad	1. 2. 3. 4. 5.						
With East	1. ✓ 2. O 3. O 4. X	n nm * e	P E C D *	N P OK *	N P OK *	VS S OK * SF	NS S OK * SF
Complex	1. 2. 3. 4.						

cratic demands but none that seem any more than compromises that have to be made solely for the sake of survival.

Here are several possibilities that a number of schools I've been working with have reluctantly considered:

1. Present a group portrait showing the percentage of students on each level before and after:

FOR EXAMPLE:

	Beginning	Not Bad	With Ease	Complex
Sept.	20	30	40	10
June	15	35	35	15

This gross portrait says nothing other than that some students learned how to read better over the year. It smacks of standardized tests, and though some people choose to use it, it seems a dangerous compromise if used to evaluate a program. After all it says nothing about why changes happened, who they happened to, what growth took place within the levels, etc.

2. Present percentages of students who showed some growth or change on one or more component.

FOR EXAMPLE:

   92% of students showed change
   8% didn't

This could be made even more specific to the point of being comic.

FOR CONFIDENCE:

   number of students on beginning level 6 change
                                          1 nothing

                           not bad level 8 change
                                          0 nothing

with ease level 12 change
                 1 nothing

complex level   6 change
                1 nothing

Confidence once acquired needn't be built up much. If you are pressured to show change as many public alternative schools are then to survive you have to manufacture the illusion of change. I can imagine the need to show change driving people to distinguish five or seven levels of "confidence" so that it is possible to claim small change when nothing is actually perceived. Group portraits, though they might keep administrators off one's back, still don't tell much about what is happening between students and teachers.

However teachers in public schools are not the only ones to blame for trying to use tests for personal justification or to displace responsibility. When kids fail to learn the administrators like to attribute it to the teachers, teachers to the parents or the kids, and the kids and parents, when they are not intimidated, want to place it back onto the teachers or administrators. No one wants to take responsibility him or herself, say he or she was wrong and go about the business of changing.*

Everyone wants to design a test to take them off the spot and say that others have failed. People do not trust each other, expect cheating, and therefore are driven to justify themselves by "objective" means.

The latest version of this cynical use of testing is to place all blame on the materials used. For example, a

---

* This applies as well to many kids who are scared to assume the responsibility for teaching themselves.

number of people in the Berkeley Unified School District have just decided to purchase an entire prepackaged reading program. The program claims to be able to teach everyone to read. It is supposed to be teacher-proof, student-proof, administrator-proof and parent-proof. That is none of them are supposed to be able to mess it up. It holds great hope for some people. But for most it solves the problem of responsibility—if the kids can't read it is the fault of the materials; no one in contact with the kids needs to be burdened with the responsibility of helping the kids learn how to read, not even themselves.

3. There is another way to provide a group portrait without falling into the trap of numbers games. It is possible to make individual profiles for all learners several times a year and use these changing profiles as indicators of change. It is also possible to give pictures of the least and most accomplished readers in a group and indicate where most of the people cluster. The decision of exactly how to do this should be left to the learners and the teaching people.

It is also possible to describe what change has taken place (or hasn't—for some people no change may be healthy at that moment in their lives) while insisting that the whole picture is merely a sketch and, therefore, that any question of detail or responsibility requires looking at all the profiles and talking to everyone involved.

Here is a sketch of how an imaginary group of twenty-five might be doing (*see facing page*).

The top line shows where one of the people having trouble is; the bottom shows one of the more successful readers. The hatched part in the middle indicates where most of

| | | Physical Condition | | Understanding | | | | |
		Stamina	Speed	Book Understanding	Street Understanding	Strategy	Confidence	Skills
Beginning		NS S OK SF	VS S OK SF	N P OK	N P OK	P E C D	n nm e	1. 2. 3. 4. 5. 6.
Not Bad		NS S OK SF	VS S OK SF	N P OK	N P OK	P E C D	n nm e	1. 2. 3. 4. 5.
With Ease		NS S OK SF	VS S OK SF	N P OK	N P OK	P E C D	n nm e	1. 2. 3. 4.
Complex		NS S OK SF	VS S OK SF	N P OK	N P OK	P E C D	n nm e	1. 2. 3. 4.

the people are. The sketch indicates that many students need to build up confidence, that speed and stamina are somewhat of a problem, but that most of the kids are street wise. There are other things one can read from the sketch but fortunately not too many. I would resist any attempts to fill in the sketch and insist that to get the full picture every person must be considered individually.

A year later the sketch of the same group might look like this (*see facing page*).

4. There are some people I have spoken to who have a need to be very specific. They have suggested another modification of the schema, which would deal with each individual component skill on all the other aspects of reading. For example, they have suggested a form like this (*see page 170*).

In other words skill number three on the not bad level is considered on all the other components. I don't like it. The whole thing is cut so fine that it becomes meaningless. Many of the components are deliberately matters of general ability and knowledge. It makes no sense to me to be so specific about street knowledge, stamina, speed, etc., with respect to every skill. I am very wary of the over-determination and overanalysis of a subject. Get as much information as is necessary to function well. There is a point at which too much specific information may confuse the learner and the teacher and interfere with learning rather than make it easier.

Skills	Confidence	Strategy	Understanding — Street Understanding	Understanding — Book Understanding	Physical Condition — Speed	Physical Condition — Stamina
Beginning 1. 2. 3. 4. 5. 6.						
Not Bad 1.✓ 2.✓ 3.O 4.O 5.O	n nm e	P E C D	N P OK	N P OK	VS S OK SF	NS S OK SF
With Ease 1. 2. 3. 4.	n nm e	P E C D	N P OK	N P OK	VS S OK SF	NS S OK SF
Complex 1.✓ 2.✓ 3.O 4.O	n nm e	P E C D	N P OK	N P OK	VS S OK SF	NS S OK SF

		Understanding				Physical Condition	
Level	Skills	Confidence	Strategy	Street Understanding	Book Understanding	Speed	Stamina
Not Bad	3.	n nm * e	P E *C D	N P *OK	N *P OK	VS *S OK SF	NS *S OK SF

CONDITION 4:
BELIEVING THAT READING
IS IMPORTANT

If you want to help others learn to read there are some questions you ought to ask yourself first:

1. Is reading important in your life, necessary for your survival or existence? How?

2. Do you enjoy reading? Do you like the smell of books or fresh print, the look of certain typefaces or letters, the feel of some books? Are your senses involved in reading as well as your head?

3. Have you learned much of use from books in your life? Has reading or writing provided you with joy, power, awareness, sensitivity? Has reading and writing been a dry, cold intellectual activity you have to force yourself to participate in? Or is it a mixed experience?

4. Why should your students learn how to read? To be able to deal with people who might try to cheat and exploit them with loan agreements, contracts, leases, laws, tests, etc.? To be able to acquire their own voice and listen to the voice of other men and women who have struggled to be free of exploitation? To take some private pleasure from books and have access to lots of stories and information? To be able to sustain a dialogue with the dead through the words they leave behind? To be able to read do-it-yourself books and gain skills?

5. How difficult do you think learning to read is? Do you believe your students can learn easily or with difficulty? Do you believe learning can take place in an instant? Do you believe there is time to learn from your students?

6. What kind of change do you like to see? How do you get rewarded for trying to teach? Is it your pupils' power, their dependence on you, money? What do you get out of it?

7. Do you think that the days of reading are over, that it is an obsolete medium that will be replaced by television or other more immediate forms of communication? Do you find reading necessary though a drag? Would you rather be teaching something else? Why don't you?

People who don't read or write themselves with any frequency or joy have a hard time getting others to read and write. It is difficult to teach people to value what you yourself do not value.

Students spend time figuring out their teachers' beliefs and usually have a pretty accurate view of them, often despite what the teachers say themselves. If you don't be-

lieve that reading and writing are important human activities your students will know it and tend to feel the same
way you do. If you don't believe your students can learn
to read with ease then the students will know that too and
question their own abilities.

The way the teacher feels about the students and the
subject are crucial elements in any teaching-learning situation.

If you do not believe young people or poor people or
black people or yellow or brown people can learn with
ease do not attempt to teach them. If you tend to look
upon people who are different than you as damaged or
inferior you can only do them harm by trying to teach
them. You will try to "elevate" them and expect them to
fail, since you have already decided that they aren't like
you.

Finally, if you believe reading is a difficult and sacred
skill most likely you will make it seem difficult and holy
to your students and create learning problems for them.
Reading and writing will be acquired naturally if you can
be natural about it and believe it is worth doing.

CONDITION 5:
READING MATERIALS

All you really need to help someone learn to read and write is something to write with and something to write on. Starting with nothing more elaborate than paper and some pencils one can:

> put down the alphabet
> write stories, jokes, tales
> develop exercises in sound combinations
> make lists and books
> create one's own curriculum out of the spoken language of the learner

Of course, if you can afford more than the bare minimum the following is a list of materials I have found useful:

1.

so students can make their own signs and posters, play with designing a page of print, make poems, etc. One should try to get as wide a variety of stamps as possible so that poems, pictures, etc., can be created. It is also possible to get stamps made up cheaply. Students can design their own signs or mottos, which can be made into stamps such as the following that I had made up:

The last four stamps—the frog, person, lock, and hacksaw—were used for a series of games called school, prison, hospital, and welfare. The students drew a board consisting of a jail, hospital, ward, or classroom; stamped the frog where the teacher or jailer was; put the person where the students or prisoners were; put locks on places that were prohibited to students or prisoners; and then made up rules for the use of the hacksaw to open locked up places. See if you can make up your own games.

2.

STENCILS

$$ \wr \, \varsigma \div + \backslash ^{o} _{o} $$

Stencils are fun to play with, cheap, and come in a wide variety of sizes. Some students who don't have the patience to do elaborate work with stamps take to stencils.

3.

```
A DYMO LABEL MAKER
```

Kids love to label objects and people, and some of the cheap label makers provide good practice for someone learning to read. Try to label things yourself—chairs, tables, desks, people's clothes, etc. Most dymo labels stick on anything and come off without leaving marks. Don't settle for simple labels. Vary them, play with them so that, for example, you might have the chairs in your room labeled:

```
THE   HOT   SEAT.          A FUNNY CHAIR
```

```
THE SEAT OF POWER
```

4. If dymo label makers are too expensive blank tags and labels are just as good and give greater opportunity for elaboration. Once I played labeling games with some

high school kids and here are some of the instructions put on different objects in the school:

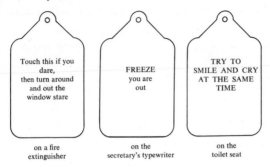

Touch this if you
dare,
then turn around
and out the
window stare

on a fire
extinguisher

FREEZE
you are
out

on the
secretary's typewriter

TRY TO
SMILE AND CRY
AT THE SAME
TIME

on the
toilet seat

5. Plastic or wooden letters. There are plastic letters that come with little magnets and a metallic board. The board and letters can be used for free play but they also can be used to illustrate how words and sounds vary. For example, using small magnets at the back of the board you can start with five letters, one in each corner and one in the middle. Then bring some together using the magnets

so the letters appear to move themselves. The following transformations can be illustrated with just these letters:

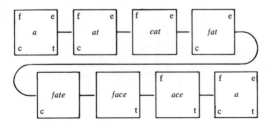

The more easily the students can function with the substitutions and additions and changes in letter order represented above, the more capable they will be of dealing easily with combinations of sounds.

6. A pair of scissors, index cards, a bottle of paper cement, as well as old newspapers and magazines. With this material it is possible to make up interesting card games as well as found poetry. For example, some sixth-graders cut the following phrases out of the *San Francisco Chronicle* and pasted them on index cards:

year of the rat	today's
back for more	the life of a
the busing issue	warning on fussing
is	attack
at ease in	
a threat of	
games in Oakland	
your land	
America's largest	
dreams of next year	
officials protest	

Then they dealt the cards around a circle and built up a poem in the following way:

The first person laid down one of the cards.

The next person added a card from his or her hand either before, after, above, or below the previous one and so on around the circle until all the cards were laid out. This is a noncompetitive game—there are no winners. Everyone works together to make a collective statement. Then the whole poem/statement can be pasted on a large sheet of paper, or the cards can be picked up, reshuffled, and another poem made.

You don't have to cut words out of a newspaper. Blank index cards can be used in the same way. Pass out five cards to each person, ask them to put any words they want on the cards, collect them, shuffle them, then deal them out again. Poems can be generated in this way and people get a chance to practice composing with words while playing the game.

7. Speedball pens and lettering charts are nice to have around. Some people love to make alphabets and copy down sayings and quotations in fancy lettering styles. The pleasure of writing things out by hand is disappearing. The ball-point pen and the typewriter provide different sensual pleasures than the lettering pen, which moves slowly and deliberately and can be controlled much more than the other two. If you are interested in the visual beauty of print, hand-lettered signs can provide a lot of pleasure.

8. Index cards can be useful in many ways. For example, I have a card file full of writing topics available for people I have helped with writing. The file, which is constantly added to by all of us, contains titles, first sentences, pictures, captions that can set someone off writing. Here are some of the topics:

> Set me on fire
> Help me if you can I'm . . .
> Pictures from a down world
> Up high

Make war with me

Make up a diary of a young $\begin{cases} \text{child} \\ \text{man} \\ \text{woman} \end{cases}$

Write out a dream of years, make the dream into a
    poem
Fear and trembling
Make peace with me
A voice in the crowd

Presents of a metaphysical sort: $\begin{cases} \text{a \_\_\_\_ for \_\_\_\_} \\ \text{and a \_\_\_\_ for \_\_\_\_} \end{cases}$

Notebook of a down person
Write a story about something that cannot be told (I
    could not tell)
I used to _____, but now I _____ (repeated)
Why? Oh God, why?
The third eye, what would it see, it can see only when
    the other two cannot see, is only open when they
    are closed
It's news
Search
Planet news
I am the man
I was _____

9. Cartoons are a great source of writing material. Cut
out the cartoons from old magazines and newspapers, remove the captions, and paste the pictures on cardboard.
Have the cartoons available for people to make up their
own captions, which can be printed up and used as reading
material.

10. If you can afford it typewriters can be useful in
helping people write and read. Primary typewriters, which

have very large letters, are particularly good. Also, some electric typewriters have no jamming keys, which is useful for younger people who tend to strike a lot of keys at the same time.

11. Tape recorders come in handy too. They can be used:

    a. to record stories, jokes, tales, poems that can later be copied down and read.

    b. to enable people to hear their reading voice in private and practice reading aloud, singing, shouting, chanting, reciting.

    c. to record books so students can listen to books spoken aloud while following along with the written text. This is great practice for beginning readers. I've thought of recording a whole library of books for kids read by other kids and making tapes available along with the books.

    d. taping things from the radio or television, or making up one's own radio or TV shows, copying down some of the material recorded to assist in the study of voice.

12. I mentioned previously that all kinds of free or inexpensive reading material can easily be obtained. A partial list includes:

billboard sections
telephone books (including the yellow pages)
old ads and signs
posters and buttons of all sizes and shapes
newspapers, magazines
street signs, comic books
catalogues

instruction manuals for appliances

road maps (free at gas stations)

drivers' manuals (free at the Bureau of Motor Vehicles)

old greeting cards

packages (cereal boxes, beer cartons, cigarette packs, matchbooks)

postage stamps (stamp collecting will teach a lot of reading)

record jackets

13. The U.S. Government Printing Office is one of the best sources of cheap well-produced books on a whole variety of technical and practical matters from farming manuals to population studies, histories of toys and planes and cars. Send away to the U.S. Government Printing Office for a catalogue. It is amazing to me that their material isn't used more.

14. Manuals; do-it-yourself books; civil service exams and high school equivalency test books; bird, plant, tree, and animal guides; travel guides—all provide rich illustrated material and should be available to your learners if possible.

15. The more books available the better. Libraries are a natural source for books if one is poor. Also, it makes sense to set up book exchanges where the teachers and learners pool all but their most treasured books. Everyone involved contributes and borrows books. Paperback exchanges are easiest to manage. If there are books that the exchange does not have and are wanted people can pool their money, buy the book collectively, take turns reading it, and let it be permanently a part of the exchange's resources.

16. I have found a number of books useful in my work helping others to read. Naturally a dictionary (I recommend the *Shorter Oxford English Dictionary* or the *American Heritage Dictionary*) and a copy of *Roget's Thesaurus* are useful. In addition to these, however, are other less familiar but equally useful books:

a. Eric Partridge's *Origins,* which is one of my favorite books. It gives the origins of words as well as their original meanings. Partridge has also put together two other useful and fun books:

Slang Today and Yesterday, Bonanza Books.
A Dictionary of Slang and Unconventional English.

b. Other interesting collections of words from our language are:

Major, Clarence, *Dictionary of Afro-American Slang,* International Publishers, 1970.
Wentworth, Harold, and Flexner, Stuart Berg, *Dictionary of American Slang,* Thomas Y. Crowell Co., 1970.

c. There are several books that help clear up points of grammar and so-called correct usage in pleasant and sensible ways. They are:

Follett, Wilson, *Modern American Usage,* Hill and Wang, Inc., 1966.
A Manual of Style, The University of Chicago Press, 1969.

This book is full of information for would-be authors, editors, and printers. It contains many illustrations of different kinds of print, as well as suggestions for the preparation of manuscripts, discussions of points of grammar, and suggestions for editors.

d. Theodore M. Bernstein has written a number of sensible and readable books about writing in the English language. The subtitle of *Miss Thistlebottom's Hobgoblins* (Farrar, Straus and Giroux, 1971), my favorite of the books, gives a good idea of their content: *The Careful Writer's Guide to the Taboos, Bugbears and Outmoded Rules of English Usage.*

e. A World Almanac is always good to have around since most people are curious about records, facts, and figures. The index of *The 1971 World Almanac and Book of Facts* published for the *San Francisco Chronicle* by Newspaper Enterprise Associates, Inc., reads like a pop poem. For example, in the middle of page 9 one finds:

Contests
      Miss Universe 320
      Miss America Pageant 321
      Miss USA 320
      Spelling Bee, Natl. 169
      Continental Congress 208, 774
      Continental Divide 663, 700
      Continental Football League . . 840
      Continents . . . .

Guessing games, quizzes, all kinds of delightful nonsense can be developed using the almanac. There is also useful information in the book and dozens of uses can be found for it.

17. A small printing press or mimeograph machine can be used for making books, printing magazines or newspapers, making stationery letterheads or notices of meetings, etc. One can develop an entire curriculum with ingenuity and a mimeograph machine.

Bookbinding equipment is a good way to involve people in becoming familiar with books as objects. For simple binding all that is needed is a stapler, glue, cardboard, and scraps of cloth. The scraps pasted on cardboard make handsome covers for books.

A saddle-stitch stapler, which is somewhat expensive (between twelve and fifteen dollars), is useful to staple pamphlets together along the spine. They turn folded paper into official-looking books.

More complex binding presses and glues, etc., are also available but not necessary.

Learning to bind books is particularly important if you are building a library of students' work since unbound material tends not to survive very long.

18. Films with captions such as the series for the deaf produced by the U.S. Office of Education as well as the film strips most schools have available make interesting and simple reading. Another way to get people to read is to show lots of foreign-language movies that have subtitles. The more interesting the films the more likely people are to work on reading the English titles.

19. A collection of sheet music or the transcribed lyrics of popular songs interest a lot of people. They can be used especially well if records are available and students can read along while listening to the music.

20. Old 45 rpm records and copies of top-ten lists also make popular reading matter. My three- and five-year-old daughters are as interested in the latest Jackson Five records as I am in the latest work of Bob Dylan or Ornette Coleman.

21. Paolo Freire uses some drawings specifically designed to get people talking about their lives and focusing on specific politically charged concepts and words. Here is an example of Freire's drawings and the questions asked about it:

1st Situation: Man *in* the world and *with* the world. Nature and Culture.

In the debate of this situation, in which man as a being of relationships is discussed, one arrives at the distinction between the two worlds—that of nature and that of culture. One perceives the normal position of man as a being in the world and with the world.

As a creating and re-creating being who, by means of work, goes about altering reality. With simple questions such as who made the well? why did he make it? how did he make it? when? which are repeated with respect to all the elements of the situation, the two basic ideas emerge: that of *necessity* and that of *work* and culture becomes explicit on the primary level, that of subsistence. Man made the well because he had the necessity of water. And he made it to the degree that, relating himself to the world, he made of it an object of his knowledge. Submitting it, through work, to a process of transformation. In the same way he made his house, his clothes, his instruments of work. From there on the group discusses, in terms clearly simple but critically objective, relationships among men, who are not able to be dominated or transformed, as the things previously discussed, but who are subjects.

A few years ago I did something somewhat similar though not as well. I had a friend draw pictures of socially charged situations such as a cop busting a kid, someone selling dope, a poor person menacing a very rich-looking individual, a politician speaking to a group of teen-agers, etc. Then I asked the kids to put captions on the pictures or figure out one word that summarized what was happening. Then I used those words and captions as focuses both for discussions of oppression and power and for the basis of reading lessons. In fact, learning to read and learning to be articulate about one's own life can be considered one activity.

22. There are many different ways to use photographs and drawings. A few years ago I made up a small portfolio, which was filled with photographs, drawings, collages. On the inside of the portfolio the following suggestions were made for the use of this visual material:

lo ok at

with your left eye
        right eye

    with the eyes of
    a dog, an ant,
    a god

look at yourself through the
    eyes of
    people
    things
        in the picture

transform yourself into them
    them into yourself

b
o
t
h

e
y
e
s

MAKE into a puzzle
DESTROY and RECONSTRUCT

put into A
newspaper
magazine

on a car passing by

PASTE on
the floor
ceiling
walls

CUT up
Fold
make INTO collages
use IN games

PLAY WITH

WRITE ABOUT

MAKE UP A STORY
        CHARACTERS
        A JOKE, A TALE, A FABLE
            SAD FUNNY TRAGIC SIMPLE COMPLEX

DESCRIBE THE SCENE
            WHAT HAPPENS BEHIND THE WINDOWS WALLS
                        ON THE NEXT STREET
                        THE NEXT DAY
                        THE DAY BEFORE

WHAT WORLD DOES THE PICTURE PRESENT?

                    BETTER
THINK OF A WORSE   ONE ...
            DIFFERENT.
        POEM
MAKE A PLAY   WITH THE PICTURE
        STORY
        MYTH

            THINK OF SOMETHING ELSE TO
                            DO
                        WITH
                            IT

some pictures to

TALK ABOUT

MAKE UP
    peopletaleseventsfablesparables

SAY
    what
        you
    seedon'tseecanseewouldliketo
                    see

what can you see and what can't you see in
        a
            picture?

PAINT

WRITE   **ON**

DRAW

    make GrAfFiTi
        draw a moustache
            a heart
                a submarine
    paint out a person
            add someone
        color it
            make a caption
            do it over again your own way......

23. It would also be possible to make up a series of reading posters to spread throughout an oppressed community in order to get people thinking about the way reading can help them achieve a voice and achieve power over their lives. Some possible posters:

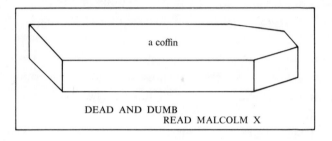

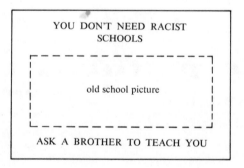

24. It might be fun and useful for people learning to read to design posters that teach about sounds and sound combinations. The usual presence of such material often does more than weeks of boring drill. For example, I can imagine a poster with the following words and appropriate illustrations:

```
COP
POP
STOP
DROP
```

```
KNOCK
SOCK
BLOCK
ROCK
```

25. Expensive reading programs have their place, I suppose. If you are in a school and are given material, use it. Some phonic workbooks might be fun or useful for some kids. Even the worst basal readers can be parodied. It helps to take the expensive, slickly produced material that is forced on you and, with the students, find ways of using it that fit your needs rather than the manual's instructions. Sometimes it is interesting to use the teacher's manual as a text with the students so you can examine together what the experts expect of teachers as well as students.

26. Scrabble, word lotto, anagrams, password, the Cities game, Blacks and Whites, and a lot of other commercially produced games require some reading and are engaging.

They do not specifically teach reading but a lot of casual experience with the printed word is picked up painlessly and indirectly while people play these games. The best analysis and list of games I know of is Sid Sackson's *A Gamut of Games* (Random House, 1969). Look through the book and see if you can incorporate some interesting games into your program.

Another way to find out about games is to wander through a toy store and check out all the games in stock. If you don't have much money see how the commercially produced games are made and then make your own version. I have seen a number of versions of Monopoly made in Berkeley based on noncapitalist principles. When you get a game modify its rules, see if you can turn it from a competitive into a collective experience, try to make it more interesting. Just as traditional reading materials can be used in many nontraditional ways the same is true for games.

27. Turn on "Sesame Street" and "The Electric Company" if they interest the students. My kids like them and have learned the alphabet and some words painlessly from watching. Don't make a big deal over them—if they're useful, OK. If not forget them.

There is no need to feel that one cannot help people learn to read without a lot of expensive material. *Use what you have, take what you can get, and make what you need.*

CONDITION 6:
THE CONTEXTS OF LEARNING

We are accustomed to thinking of learning to read as an activity that occurs in school. That need not be the case and in this section a variety of different learning contexts ranging from the classroom to the living room will be considered.

LEARNING TO READ IN A NATURAL MANNER
WITHIN A CLASSROOM
OR THE OPEN CLASSROOM REVISITED

The so-called open classroom has developed as an attempt to change individual self-contained classrooms (or a small group of classrooms within large schools) without necessarily changing the whole school or the culture the schools embody. Because of the modest goals of open classrooms they have come under fire from people who believe that nothing less than a total redistribution of wealth and power and a redefinition of culture will eliminate oppression, racism, and exploitation. I agree that our goal must be such redistribution and redefinition yet find that different people choose different battlefields. Some people can work effectively outside of the public school system; others are most effective building from within their isolated classrooms, keeping in mind however that the goal of open education is not to make life more comfortable for a chosen few students, but to provide a group of students with the strength and ability to devote their lives to creating a human, just, and equitable society. Therefore, an "open classroom"—of the sort I envisage anyway—will not be a self-indulgent individualistic collection of isolated students so much as a socialistic humanist community in miniature.

Let me elaborate on the role of the teacher and student in an open setting:

The classroom as a unit consisting of students and a teacher sharing a room in which learning is supposed to take place is a common basis of traditional and most open classroom settings. However there are significant differences in the cultural and social forms of existence within these settings. In an open classroom the teacher is not the initiator of all activity and does not run a competitive game in which the students are forced to participate. Rather the teacher has the responsibility for creating an interesting learning environment for students to explore and use; for being available to answer questions and provide resources students request; and for suggesting and presenting options to students so they can have a sense of what it is possible to learn. This last responsibility of an adult in an open classroom is crucial. Many people have interpreted the role of the adult in an open learning setting as more passive than I see it. The adult is not merely there to create an environment and step out of the way, letting the kids "do their own thing." He or she must care about the students learning certain skills and have ideas about how young people can go about acquiring them. The adult has to be willing to make suggestions, offer advice, question the students, sometimes push them, at other times leave them alone. Whether kids learn and participate in activities should not be a matter of indifference to the adults involved. They should care whether their students read or count in the same way that they would care about whether their own children walk or talk. Though adults cannot compel young people to learn and create learning problems when they try, that does not mean that adults should not try to encourage young people to learn. Ideally the adult should embody a humane, full way of living and invite the students to become part of a sane cooperative culture. This means offering the young ways of becoming competent and skillful adults.

I have often thought in this context of how certain native American peoples bring their young into the culture. First they provide living examples in their daily lives of caring for life, of respecting each other and the land they work on, and of living cooperatively. Then they give the young tools of the adult culture—farm implements, musical instruments, weapons, etc., and tell the kids to come on in. If the culture is enriching the young will welcome the opportunity to take part. It is when the culture is hypocritical, inhuman, exploitative, ugly as is our culture that the young turn away from the old and want no part of the dominant culture. At this point alternative culture forms must grow if we are not to become isolated, despairing, nodding, disconnected people.

The open setting within a school is one modest way of providing an alternative, cooperative, self-fulfilling culture for some young people. To make this work, however, the adult in the classroom must be able to cooperate, must have overcome his or her own racist, competitive, authoritarian tendencies. This is no easy role for an adult in our culture. It is easier to become an individualist, to concentrate on individual growth and development within the context of our culture than to deal with sharing. Yet people who cannot share knowledge, experience, and things are not open to each other. They hold back, hoard. I have found that the most difficult and underemphasized aspect of open education is the collective aspect. Sometimes it seems impossible to get young people to listen to each other, to teach or assist each other, to share books and food, to care about and respect each other's lives. It is not enough that individual students be free to learn at their own rates and in the manner most natural to them. The classroom is a social microcosm and it is crucial how students function with each other, what they know or care about each other's lives, what responsibility they take for each other's learning, what they consider private and what they are willing to share.

Consider learning how to read. In a collective situation students would naturally help each other, would read stories to each other, ask each other for help, share insights. They would need to look to the adult for help as a last resort.

Groups of six and seven children would find it natural to read out loud, to study the same book. The quickest student would not be looked on as the teacher's pet and a betrayer of other students, but rather as a valuable resource for the group. The slowest person would not be regarded as dumb so much as someone who needed extra time.

The crucial thing about learning to read in an open-cooperative setting is that the students would be generous toward each other and learning to read would be a collective activity like learning the latest dance or tune. I've watched kids teaching each other new dances or new dance steps. Since popular dancing is not a school subject the students do not act like traditional teachers. They dance the step themselves, walk through it, help others get the rhythm. They practice together and often show amazing patience. Anyone who knows a new step becomes a teacher for that step. There are no permanent teachers though it is usually acknowledged that some kids are better dancers than others. The worse dancers are sometimes cajoled into participating and sometimes kids are cruel to each other, but for the most part they go out of their way to save their friends unnecessary embarrassment. They act as a group though they acknowledge and appreciate individual talent. A sensible balance between the individual and collective aspects of learning is hard to achieve. However, it can be developed in a context where people respect and trust each other and this can happen in an individual classroom.

The reading program described before in this book would fit well into an open-cooperative setting. It is, however, up to each group of teachers and students to decide how they should best go about the business of helping everyone in the group learn how to read.

TEACHING READING ON THE STREETS

I have often imagined myself becoming a hobo reading teacher and letter writer. Then I could set up on the streets, in parks, on basketball courts, in a marketplace, on a lawn, in front of a school and offer reading lessons and writing services. The scribe traditionally played a similar role in countries that were not so overschooled as ours.

From my experience tutoring people in reading it seems that two hours a week for about six months can provide enough skill for people to read on a level equal to their verbal understanding.

Teaching reading away from the institutional setting of school may make it easier to undo damage school has done to many people. It may also bring reading into the daily life of a community where the schools seem like representatives of a foreign imperial power.

Here are a few possibilities for wandering reading teachers:

1. Set up a card table near where people are playing cards or dominoes and work with small groups of adults or kids. Set up exercises using words from the immediate environment or politically charged words. Leave posters behind as well as material people can use for practice.

2. Use a park bench in a similar way and work with groups of five or six people. Use letter writing as a way to engage people in discovering their own voices and writing for themselves.

3. Attach yourself as a reading teacher to some group that is doing political or social action. Use the political, social, or educational issues involved as the basis upon which you build the reading program. For example, if you

are involved in a Welfare Rights' group a natural list of
words to begin with would be:

Welfare Rights	Wrongs
Investigator	Troublemaker
Community	Power
Threat	Prison
Organize (organization, organized)	

In addition to helping people take command of the
language that affects their lives, provide services with skills
you have. Learn how to write proposals, silk-screen posters,
make handbills and comic books, use a printing press and
mimeograph machines. Learn skills that make you useful
to the community you serve—and when offering your skills
be sensitive to your role as a stranger. The best thing
would be for the teacher of reading to be a member of the
community.

4. Teach others to teach reading. If you are not a member of the community that needs a hobo teacher you probably can serve best by giving your skills and knowledge to
others who are more intimately involved in the community.

Anyone who can read can teach others to teach reading
as well as he or she does. Help the process along if you
can. Help people become courageous enough to want to
teach and generous enough to share what they know.

LITERARY CENTER

Open a storefront whose specific intent is to help people
learn how to read. Don't become a school. Provide a service
to people of all ages. Define the service as broadly as pos-

sible to include teaching printing and poster-making skills, propaganda and media techniques, etc. And once again if you do not live in a community and have no prospects of becoming a part of it, train members of the community to do what you do and phase yourself out.

LEARNING TO READ AT HOME

It should be possible for young people to learn to read at home just as they learn walking and talking for the most part at home. The following conditions would probably be all that was necessary:

1. books read aloud to young children on a regular basis
2. pencils and paper (or crayons) for them to experiment with
3. a sample alphabet
4. a collection of everyday words
5. someone to dictate their stories to
6. someone who could read and was willing to answer questions about reading
7. a relaxed and patient attitude toward learning to read so that kids wouldn't be pressed too much and become nervous about reading

If people learning how to read in a natural way were themselves encouraged to help others, especially in their own homes, the process of bringing beginning reading into the context of the home could begin. One way to undercut racist and oppressive schools is to take away their supposed reason for existing. Teach reading and math on the streets and in the home and then schools will be left without content to teach. Their actual purposes—i.e., to teach obedience, consumption, competition within a capitalist framework, and oppression—will be exposed for what they are. If the schools continue to exist with just those functions at least the battle will be clearer.

CONDITION 7:
RESPECTING THE LANGUAGE
AND CULTURE OF THE LEARNER

If there is to be a natural transition from speaking to reading the learner's voice should be present in writing as well as speech. However, in our intolerant culture some variations of the English language are judged to be superior to others. For example, so-called Standard English is said to be more expressive, abstract, powerful, proper, and correct than the dialect Blacks or Chicanos or East Europeans or Italians or Chinese speak. The grammatical forms of Standard English are looked upon as "the correct way of speaking and writing" and other forms are considered primitive and incorrect by many teachers. For example, "I am happy" is considered "correct" and "I be happy" or "I happy" are supposed to be signs of illiteracy. However, all three sentences are equally clear and expressive. There are certain myths about standard and proper language that must be set aside once and for all:

Myth 1. There is a single correct way of writing and talking. This myth translated really says that the people who make the rules in the culture want to regulate language and insist that the way they speak is better than the way others speak. One frequently hears people claim that everyone *must* learn to read and write Standard English. That statement is true only insofar as the people in power insist that official documents, job applications, business letters, etc., must be written in Standard English as a sign of conformity to the basic competitive values of the culture.

Myth 2. Some languages are more complex, abstract, and expressive than others. This is just false, though it comforts some people to believe that their way of speaking is more abstract and intellectual than that of other people. All languages known are capable of the same expressiveness and have similar structural complexity. However, how people use their language is a social and moral matter. The way people choose to use a language and the capacity of the language itself should not be confused.

Myth 3. Within a language some dialects are superior to others. This again expresses the need of one group of people to feel superior to others. Actually there is probably not even a functioning "standard dialect." There are a wide variety of ways people use and pronounce the English language within our society and these variations have to do with the original languages people spoke as well as the social class of the speakers and the part of the country they came from. It is important to eliminate linguistic imperialism and understand that the imposition of a standardized language is just another form of oppression. This is not to deny, however, that people ought to compromise enough to make their writing comprehensible to the audience they want to reach.

Myth 4. If people learn to read and write in their own dialect they will never learn the standard language. This again is a major put-down of poor or minority people. It is no big deal to be able to read and write in so-called Standard English as well as in one's own natural voice, especially for someone who understands something about reading and language. After all one can understand many dialects with ease, imitate them in speech, and consequently in writing. Anyone, for example, who has been exposed to television has heard a lot of so-called standard ways of talking and can imitate many television characters. One can learn to read and write in a number of dialects at the same time.

Respecting the language and culture of the learner implies taking a nonelitis attitude toward language.* It implies that one does not believe that one's own way of speaking is superior as well as that one is curious about understanding the structure of other dialects. These last remarks are specifically addressed to white middle-class people. It is fashionable to be interested in so-called non-Standard English, in Black or Chicano or Puerto Rican dialect in a condescending paternalistic way. I have seen many young teachers who say they believe that kids should be allowed to speak and write in their own dialects. The tone these teachers take implies that the natives should be

* *Black English* by J. L. Dillard (Random House, 1972) substantiates the points made in this section with respect to the speech of Black Americans. It should be read by anyone who thinks about language and culture.

indulged a bit before being raised to the level of "our language." One has to listen to how people speak, to think about language, to be aware of how one's own values slip into so-called objective statements about language, in order to undo the racist sense of the superiority of white middle-class language that is part of the legacy of American education.

Let me say once more: To respect someone's language does not merely mean to tolerate it or condescendingly accept it. Respect is an attitude that exists among peers, equals. It is the basis of dialogue between different peoples and different cultural traditions. Without respect in this sense it is not possible to avoid master-slave mentality.

A note on basic skills, natural learning, and different cultural traditions:

Many people make the argument that poor and minority people cannot afford humane, open, cooperative education. They claim that the basic need for poor people is to acquire the skills of reading, writing, and math, and that any non-traditional schooling will deprive them of skills needed to survive and therefore perpetuate their powerlessness. I find this attitude condescending and patronizing. Poor students, minority students, people, respond when they are respected. One of the main points of this book is to show that the skills of reading and writing can be obtained by all people in humane, natural, open ways. Another point is that the learning situation has to be tailored to the culture and lives of the students. There are and should be open learning situations that exist within the setting of Black, Chicano, Puerto Rican, Appalachian culture. There is no question in my mind that it is necessary for people in our culture to be able to read and write. The question is how people acquire those skills and what else they learn on the way.

An interesting situation developed in Berkeley a few years ago. According to the test results taken as a whole, Berkeley was a bit above the mythical national norm. When the scores were broken down, as they were three years ago at the insistence of a few members of the black community, it was discovered that there was a bimodal distribution of scores within the city. The white kids were well above the norm, and the black kids were below. Whatever one's feeling about testing, the results indicated one thing clearly—in terms of the school and society the white kids were making it, and the black kids were not.

The test results also revealed in a crude way something else which could not be ignored—the white kids could read and the black kids couldn't. Something had to be done, and here is where the conflict came in.

There was a cry for a reemphasis on basic skills within the school district. Many white kids and parents did not favor this since their kids already had those skills and needed other things from school. However, there was another and unfortunately little noticed contradiction: Some conservative members of the black community were asking the teachers to reemphasize the basics when, in fact, the way they had been emphasized in the past was precisely what had led to failure. In the panic over scores, issues like teacher accountability were bandied about. Finally, a formula (later not enforced) was developed and approved by the school board, where each teacher was to be held accountable for one year's growth in reading for each student in his or her class. There was naturally a general panic and a harsh reemphasis on phonics and all the other pseudoprofessional paraphernalia of the teaching profession. Failure was built into the situation, for black kids do not easily succeed in the cultural world of white middle-class schools.

At a meeting of administrators I was asked what the school I ran would do about the board mandate. I replied that there was no problem for me in getting our students to read as long as it was left open as to how it was to be done.

The question of the need to acquire basic skills is often confused with the question of how these skills are to be acquired. I know many people who equate open education with indifferent education and believe that a teacher in an open situation does not care whether young people learn or not. Nothing could be farther from the truth. I would even go so far as to say that open education grew out of a concern for the way in which young people learn and an awareness of how present school teaching discourages learning. I want all kids to read and write, but I do not believe that all young people should be forced through a developmental reading program at the age of six and should be considered failures if that way of learning how to read is not natural to them. Young people will learn to read and calculate when the need is obvious to them and when the atmosphere in which they learn is comfortable, and when the culture of the school is natural to them.

CONDITION 8:
PATIENCE AND PRACTICE
AND A STYLE OF ONE'S OWN

What is the best age to learn how to read? Some people feel the earlier the better. I am not so sure. In my experience kids who have not learned to read by the age of eleven or twelve can pick up reading in a few months with no loss of skill or interest. The same is true of adults. On the other hand, I see no reason to discourage people from reading at any time in their lives. It will be sensible to expose young people to print as often as possible and as early as possible, and offer to teach them as much as they feel ready to learn. If young people were read to, if their questions about reading were answered, if books seemed interesting to them, and if they were able to have their own stories copied and available to read, most young people would probably pick up reading by the time they were eleven or twelve at the outside without much adult prodding. It is adult impatience, anxiety, condescension, and anger that makes reading a problem for some young people.

It is important for people who care to help others learn to read to have patience and understand that the crucial thing for learners is to learn as much as possible how to teach themselves.

There is a dangerous recent development in professional education circles that makes patience on the part of the teacher very difficult. It could be called the Great-American-School-Spy System. Teachers are supposed to break down the subject they are teaching into the smallest possible parts, all of which must be defined in terms of student behavior that can be observed and measured. Educational experts, in their zeal to evaluate teachers and have everything in the schools under control, have developed schemes so that everything a student is supposed to be learning can be described in concrete terms on a day-by-day basis. It is a fool's game. The crucial thing about learning is the development of a personal style and the ability to deal with the unfamiliar. As long as students are not trusted and are observed and measured at every moment more of their energy will be directed to getting around the system or playing with it than to gaining the skill needed to free themselves of teachers.

Students can learn how to practice in private. They can learn to rehearse skills by themselves rather than subject themselves to teacher-directed drill. I know my own children love to go off and write the letters and words they know while they are alone. Being watched by adults often bothers them.

Instead of assigning homework I have found it useful to give my students a list of things they can do by themselves or with a few friends to help them learn reading. For example, I have shown kids how to play word games like hangman or Scrabble; have given them lists of activities they could do at home or on the streets such as the following:

1. Copy down all the words you see on the way home.
2. Make a map of your apartment and label all the parts.
3. Make a family tree writing down all the names of all of your relatives you know of.
4. List all your friends and put down their astrological signs.
5. Make a map of your block complete with street signs.
6. Read your birth certificate, your brother or sister's high school yearbook.
7. Make up a yearbook listing your friends and using such categories as name, favorite record, best dance, nickname, sign, etc.

There is another aspect of teaching oneself that many students never encounter and is important. People do not know how to make themselves comfortable while learning. In school everyone is supposed to work in silence while sitting at a desk. When I write there is always some music on. I pace; like a fountain pen; write on eight-and-a-half-by-eleven-inch yellow pads with a margin on the left. I also function best in the morning. Friends of mine who write professionally and obsessively have other habits. Some type, others feel at ease with ball-point pens. Some write in cafés, others on buses or airplanes or while sitting on park benches. Evening is the best time for some people, midnight or two or three in the morning is the most productive time for others. Pads, notebooks, poster paper, lined paper, unlined paper—these all have different appeal to different writers. The same is true with reading. There are some people who cannot concentrate with music on, others who cannot concentrate without it. Some read best lying down or reclining in an easy chair, others need a straight-back chair and a table to rest the book on. Many people never realize that they are free to discover their most comfortable way of reading and writing and try to reproduce the sterile conditions of school when they try to get down to reading and writing. I know some nervous parents, for example, who insist that their children cannot read or study while the radio is on and then wonder why reading and studying are such unpleasant experiences for their kids. At this moment I am listening to some Afro-Cuban music, sitting at my desk, which is full of papers and books, smoking a cigar, and writing. Every five minutes I get up and pace. That's how I write best. It would be comical if I felt everyone had to write that way.

It is important that kids have a little space at home to work and that they be given the respect to develop their own most comfortable ways of working. A corner is sometimes all that is needed. People can work comfortably in the most crowded places if they are given the opportunity to carve out for themselves a way of functioning. The same is true for classrooms no matter how confined. Many people can work together in different manners and styles if they respect each other and understand that they are free to function as comfortably as is consistent with collective survival.

This means of course that people will have to be sensitive to each other's needs and find ways of indulging their own styles so that they do not oppress others. For example, if five people must share a room and they all want to write to music and all want to hear different music, adjustments will have to be made. Earphones can be used. If there is only one radio available then the station can be changed every hour, or people can work at different times, etc. Again the issue is balancing the personal with the collective without destroying either.

CONDITION 9:
BEING ABLE TO USE LANGUAGE

Learning to speak or communicate in sign language is a more complicated activity than learning to read. Yet most people have mastered the basic ability to use some language system by the time they are four or five. They can make up sentences as well as understand combinations of words they have never heard before. They can speak correctly according to the system they have learned, can translate ideas into sounds. They have a sense of what combinations of sounds and words are nonsense according to the language they know and have mastered the ability to express their wants and needs and feelings to others in a socially agreed upon way.

The ability to read is based upon the ability to speak and involves many of the same skills. Reading should present no problem to people who have learned to speak. However there are some people who do not learn how to communicate. Sometimes a person's brain or senses are so damaged that he or she cannot master any system of communication. Nevertheless the damage has to be pretty serious for the human brain not to be able to compensate for the disability. The blind can speak. The deaf have developed a language of signs. People are driven to communicate with each other for the sake of survival.

If a person can master a complex system of communication such as a language (including sign language), he or she should be able to learn how to read in that language. Occasionally there are people who speak with ease but who have trouble remembering signs or putting signs together with sounds. These people need special sense training and perhaps it will take them longer to learn how to read than others. But with time, patience, and a good measure of common sense and ingenuity all but the most damaged people can learn how to read.

However there are ways to create reading problems for people with minor perceptual problems. There is a tendency in our culture to overclassify problems of learning and turn them into diseases. For example, in recent educational literature there is a new category of learning problems called "perceptual disorders." Under this heading fall such false diseases as aphasia, dysgraphia, and dyslexia. In plain language a person with aphasia is someone who has trouble putting sounds together into words; someone with dysgraphia has trouble learning how to write; and someone with dyslexia has trouble translating reading marks on a page as sounds and words.

It is almost predictable that these problems with speaking, writing, and reading have given rise to a class of professionals who specialize in them as well as to elaborate and expensive remedial programs, diagnostic clinics, and a whole culture surrounding these so-called diseases.

A person who has difficulty reading can be diagnosed as having dyslexia, sent to a professional, put in an elaborate program of sense training, and treated generally as if he or she were sick. If the person is somewhat nervous to begin with he or she may end up believing there is something fundamentally wrong with him or her and become a serious learning problem.

It is important to avoid treating any problem of learning as a disease. If students have trouble fixing their eyes on the printed page help them with that. If they have a hard time coordinating their hands and eyes and therefore find it difficult to write, give them methods to help themselves. Be specific about people's problems. Don't mystify them and produce false explanations or big empty words. If you don't know what to do admit it and try to figure out a way to approach the problem with your students. A basic responsibility of people who care to teach is to be honest and direct with their students and assume responsibility for what they don't know. It is false and damaging to dress up one's own ignorance with professional or scientific language.

CONDITION 10:
THE SO-CALLED PROBLEM
OF MOTIVATION

In my experience as a teacher I have not met a young person who didn't want to learn how to read. I have met young people who believed they were too dumb to learn, or who were too nervous to approach books. There are youngsters who have been damaged by their school experience and pretend that reading is stupid or useless, yet they too want the power of adults and part of that power in our culture is the ability to read.

A lot of teachers complain that their students aren't motivated to read. That is like complaining that the students aren't motivated to walk or talk or run or dance or play. In many classrooms students are not motivated to talk or sing; they do not want to subject themselves to the teacher's power to correct them or declare them wrong or inferior. Many black kids do not for example want to talk to white middle-class teachers who look down upon Afro-American dialects. These kids are sometimes declared nonverbal because they don't want to talk to that particular teacher.

The problem of motivation is a false problem. There is no need to motivate people to grow and reading is part of growing in our culture. What might be necessary is negating the students' previous learning experiences. Sometimes it is important to randomize things or stand them on their heads so that old fears can be overcome. For example, it helps to find out how someone was taught in the past and then do the opposite. It helps to remove learning from the classroom, to find friends that can share knowledge, to build from everyday experience rather than a textbook.

It also helps to have a sense of humor about learning. After all, the seriousness with which some people approach the process of reading is laughable. What should be easy and natural, a source of pleasure and power, can be turned into a grim and tedious chore that makes no sense to the learner and therefore destroys motivation. The situation reminds me of a singing class I observed recently. The students were seated in front of a grim-faced teacher who was repeating in a sing-song voice the words of some choral piece composed for school children. Most of the kids were obeying the teacher's commands and singing when she said sing, repeating the words when she said repeat, keeping quiet when she said silence. The singing was awful—off key, expressionless, unmusical in every way. Yet I know most of these kids—they sing well and joyously at home and on the streets, their voices are true and full of expression. There is no need to motivate them to sing, yet if school was the only experience they had with music there surely would be a problem of motivation. In the same way reading is a problem for young people only if we—the adults who already read—make it a problem.

A FINAL NOTE

If you are interested in using some of the material in this book try it on yourself first. Write the poems, play the games, do the exercises, analyze your own reading skills. Make up new games, collect resources, listen to people read. Then if you know someone who has difficulty with reading, offer help. Look around your community and discover how you can be of use. Don't wait to be asked. Plunge in and share what you know. Learn how to help and to teach others by doing.

INDEX

INDEX

About the Author

HERBERT KOHL is the author of *36 Children* and *The Open Classroom*. A graduate of Harvard and a former director of the Teachers and Writers' Collaborative, a group which attempted to revise the curriculum in elementary and secondary schools, Mr. Kohl taught and directed an open school in Berkeley, California called Other Ways, within the Berkeley Unified School District. He is a former columnist for *Grade Teacher Magazine* and was involved with parents in Harlem and East Harlem who are engaged in the struggle for community participation in education.